# Consultative Budgeting

# Consultative Budgeting

## How to Get the Funds You Need From Tight-Fisted Management

### Mack Hanan

**American Management Association**

New York • Atlanta • Boston • Chicago • Kansas City • San Francisco • Washington, D.C.
Brussels • Mexico City • Tokyo • Toronto

This publication is designed to provide accurate and
authoritative information in regard to the subject matter covered.
It is sold with the understanding that the publisher is not
engaged in rendering legal, accounting, or other professional
service. If legal advice or other expert assistance is required, the
services of a competent professional person should be sought.

Library of Congress Cataloging-in-Publication Data

Hanan, Mack.
   Consultative budgeting : how to get the funds you need from tight-fisted
management / Mack Hanan.
      p.   cm.
   Includes bibliographical references and index.
   ISBN 0-8144-0257-7
   1. Budget in business.   I. Title.
HG4028.88H35   1994
658.15'4—dc20                                                      94-13208
                                                                         CIP

Printing number

10   9   8   7   6   5   4   3   2   1

To Lew Platt of Hewlett-Packard,
for Platt's Principle for Getting Funds:

Their eyes close over when you talk
  Technology. But they open again—
So do their pocketbooks—when you prove
  The return on their investment.

## Other AMACOM books by Mack Hanan:

*Consultative Selling*™
*Competing on Value*
*Growth Partnering*
*Manage Like You Own It*
*Profits Without Products*
*Tomorrow's Competition*

# Contents

# Preface

## Coming Home on a Deal and a Prayer

The word comes down from upstairs just before lunch, killing appetites: If you plan to present a budget more than 2 to 3 percent over a year ago—the inflation rate—don't bother. You won't have a prayer.

Crisis proves unifying. Customary competitiveness among the managers, all going after the same funds, gives way to collegial concern. "How do they expect us to stay on top of best practices?" one manager asks. "At two to three percent, I'm just keeping up. And the Old Man is always saying, 'keeping up is going backwards.' "

"Why spend money on benchmarking?" another manager says. "By the time we get a real budget—if we ever do— we'll be so far behind the technology curve that the view of our competitors' rear ends will never change."

"Putting a cap on growth is one thing," a third manager adds puckishly. "But ruling out prayer—that's sacrilege. What are we supposed to do on our way upstairs, whistle 'Dixie'?"

What do you do when you can't manage any leaner or meaner? When you can't go any further back to basics because you are already operating as basic as you can get? When you can't cut costs any more without cutting quality or productivity? When all the outsourceable operations are outsourced and all the integratable systems are integrated?

"You ask for more money," a fourth manager says. "But you ask for it without asking for it, if you know what I mean."

Two weeks later, he makes clear what he means.

"What if," he asks the Old Man and the executive committee,

"we can increase our contribution to business unit profits by $3.5 million from savings over the next twelve months—$3.5 million that you can start allocating right now for next year's spending . . . $3.5 million that is the equivalent of an extra ninety days of gross sales revenues . . . $3.5 million that comes out of $1.5 million of cost reduction from reduced downtime and the other $2 million results from decreasing scrap, rework, and repairs under warranty?"

He has their attention. "What if the $3.5 million represents an approximate fifteen percent rate of return on your investment, which will be paid back by month seven of year one?"

So this is how you go for funds without going for funds, the other managers think to themselves. Instead of asking for money, you offer money—more money than you want to get.

Later, the manager shares his secrets. "I put management in the position of having to turn down *my money,* not turn down my request for *their money.* I appeal to them as investors, not as philanthropists or the last of the big-time spenders. I make them hold out their hands to me rather than the other way around. From the first words out of my mouth, I get them thinking about the $3.5 million I can get *for* them and not how much I came up here to get *from* them."

"So you turn a request for appropriations into . . . what?" asks one of the other managers.

"A bequest of incremental profits. A new source of cash flow. A business deal."

"What do you do if they say 'Thanks, but no thanks. We have a better deal.' "

"I come back up with an even better deal."

"How many times do you come back up?"

"Until they won't have a prayer if they wait any longer to invest their money with me and let me put it to work. I make the time value of money work for me. 'Look at how much you're losing out on every day you put off investing in my proposal,' I tell them. If you don't make a decision for whatever number of days, you will already have paid an opportunity cost for this or that percent of the benefits without having the benefits. Plus, the ongoing problems will continue to put us at a competitive disadvantage."

The manager takes on a holy look. "Think of it as my small contribution to keeping prayer alive in corporate America."

# Consultative Budgeting

# *Introduction*

# Changing the Way You Go for Funds

"Get funded or die a slow death" has always been a manager's mantra. Before the 1990s, when top managers wanted to keep everything in-house, even bad managers got funded so that their operations would not die. Today, top management has a new option: They can kill you instantly by outsourcing your operation to a more cost-effective source of supply as a better use of what is often a lesser amount of their funds and the time and talent required to oversee them.

The outsource option creates a vicious circle for you. The novelty rate of new technology is continually going up. Unless you can exceed your traditional hit ratio of getting appropriations requests funded, you will be unable to keep up with competition in developing and applying technology. This will cause you to fall behind, preventing you from achieving best practices, without which you are an impediment rather than a contributor to competitiveness; in other words, you are a prime target for outsourcing.

Top management has no choice. Neither do you. You must be able to source the funds to finance your strategic operations at or ahead of the novelty rate. Every manager's new mantra must be "Source or be outsourced."

Selling your appropriations requests upstairs has become a matter of professional survival. The old attitudes of "win some, lose some" or "you can't win them all" are no longer affordable. If you miss a curve, the one you lose out on can put you out of business. Your appropriations hit rate and the novelty rate of innovation in your industry must become one-to-one.

The traditional selling skills of operating managers in going for funds are no longer sufficient. Current skills—"skill currency"—are more of an impediment than an enabler. Every day managers lose out, and their businesses lose out along with them, because inherently productive proposals for funds are turned down on a manager's inability to do two things:

1. Fit an operating project to one of top management's strategic business objectives so that they can buy into it as a business decision.
2. Convert a request for funds into a proposal to contribute new funds so that top management can see the business benefits along with the benefits in operating performance.

*Business fit* and *business benefits* are the two secrets for selling upstairs. It is easy to see why this is so if you put on top management's hat and look at their world—and how they see your world—through their objectives.

## Feeding the Cash Machine

The men and women upstairs—the chief officers who oversee your operation and finance it—have one thing foremost on their minds day in and day out: *making money*. No matter what business they are in, they think of it as a money machine that makes money when it sells something and makes more money when it puts the money it makes to work.

The money that a money machine takes in generates positive cash flow. When the money is put to work, it goes out and cash flow becomes negative. Some of the cash flow that goes out never comes back; it becomes a sunk cost. Other cash flows yield returns that exceed their cost; they become investments. The sooner an investment is paid back, the sooner its funds can be reinvested in the money machine to make more money. Investments get funded first. Costs, except for keeping in compliance when the alternative is being shut down or going to jail, have to fight for every dollar.

Which are you—an investment or a cost? You can tell how top management perceives you by what happens when you go for funds. Here are three sets of questions that will give you the answer:

1. Cash that goes out is justifiable only by a greater amount of cash that it can bring in—in other words, by its investment quality. The greater the amount of money returned for every dollar put out and the faster it comes back in, the higher the quality of an investment. *How high is the investment quality of your requests for funds?*

2. Putting money out is always a risk. There are no sure things. Except for a few "no-brainers," top managers can never be 100 percent certain that they will recover an investment. Over and above recovery, they never know if they will make money on it or how much they will make or how soon they will make it. Even no-brainers can carry hidden surprises. Everything that top management does in running a business is designed to reduce their risk of making bad investments—to help them be more certain that they will be paid back on time and that they will get each dollar of return over and above payback that they have bargained for. *How much risk is associated with funding you?*

3. Every operation in a business must contribute to revenues. No business is run to control costs, yet cost control is essential to ensure that maximum positive cash flow can be retained. Cost control is important to management in two ways: to avoid or reduce as many dollars of cost as possible and to contribute as many dollars of revenue as possible for each dollar of cost. The greater the productivity of each dollar of cost in generating revenue, the easier it is to get funded. *How important are you to top management's commitment to control costs? How much cost can you save for every dollar you get funded? How much revenue can you help to generate for each dollar of funds?* The more costs you save or the more revenues you contribute to, the more funds you can claim.

You can extend the same thinking to dealing with the suppliers you do business with. They come to you for funds the same way that you go upstairs: They propose and you dispose. You can play top management's role with them by requiring that they contribute positive cash flow and not just products and services. How much cost can they help you take out of a function in your operation that they sell into? How much more revenue can they help you contribute? By how much will their return on your funds exceed the funds you allocate to do business with them? Instead of submitting a bid, ask them to propose their improved profit contribution so that you can position them in their proper place on the value-added chain shown in Figure I-1.

*Management puts its money where its return is.* At the office, you get if you give. When you go upstairs to sell your proposals for

**Figure I-1.** Value-added chain.

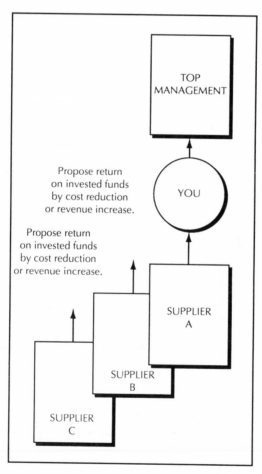

funds, make sure that you bring with you a promissory note in the form of a proposal to improve profits that will return even more money than you ask for.

As a manager, you are known upstairs by the returns you bring:

- *How much* you typically return on every dollar of funds
- *How soon* you typically return it
- *How sure* management can be about your ability to repeat your typical "muchness" and "soonness" with each new proposal

When your top managers look at you, they see you as an amalgam of muchness, soonness, and sureness. How you net out is the steak when it comes to getting funded. Everything else is the parsley around the steak.

## Letting Your Return Speak for You

Getting funded makes you top management's steward. Putting their money to work requires a different skill-set than putting a labor force to work or applying a technology or processing raw materials. Money is unforgiving. You cannot redeploy it easily once it is committed nor, because it has time value, can you reclaim your original investment if it turns out to be unproductive. A lost opportunity to make money is lost forever.

In addition, you cannot stockpile money without losing its value. A dollar invested today is always worth more to you than the same dollar invested tomorrow, even in the same project. Its perishability makes money a depreciating asset until it is put to work. Even then, you can incur an opportunity cost in the event that you could have produced a greater return, or a quicker or surer one, if you had put it to work somewhere else.

Top managers worry about these things. A wrong decision not only throws scarce funds down a rat hole, but also deprives someone else of the chance to use them better. The combination of direct loss and the loss of being able to cash in on a better opportunity makes management a two-time loser with every decision it blows.

Each allocation of funds confronts management with this double jeopardy.

Management can learn from its mistakes, but it cannot get its tuition back. What is management learning from you? Are you normally a good risk? Or having been once bitten by you, will management be twice shy? If you are a good money manager or a bad one, you make it easy for management. If you are in between, your good investments will be discounted by the bad ones. As Don Regan used to say about his managers at Merrill Lynch, "You can't have a good year one year and a bad year the next year and still have a job the year after."

It is no different at Ford, where the three most important characteristics of a manager are reliability, reliability, and reliability in such things as saving $1.50 worth of costs with every dollar in funds or helping realize three dollars in revenues with every dollar invested. Two good years do not make a career but one bad year can end one. Management simply cannot afford the risk that one bad year deserves another. By that time, all the profits from the good years will be used up by the bad ones.

Based on the facts of life "upstairs," you must change the way you go for funds in six ways:

1. *You must stop making appropriations requests.* You must bring money with you when you go upstairs, not ask for it. You must be a contributor to improved profits rather than a consumer.
2. *You must position your request for funds as an investment, not a cost.* You must be a money manager as well as an operations manager.
3. *You must sell management on acquiring returns on their investments, not on making investments.* You must present the return's dollar value and time value before you present its cost.
4. *You must get out in front of where funds are flowing.* You must fit into a strategic business objective because funds follow fit.
5. *You must prove the asset-conserving sureness of your return, not the eye-popping innovative nature of the investment.* You must reduce management's risk in doing business with you.

6. <u>*You must be a consistent producer of profit-improving outcomes,*</u> <u>*not a spotty, hit-or-miss performer.*</u> You must emphasize your reliability.

If all this seems like radical change to you, there are still lots of ways to get around valuing your proposals. You can take the point of view that top management is going to have to spend a certain amount of money on your operation just to keep competitive, so why bother measuring your contributions. Or you can look at the time it takes to assess your values as diverting you from what you really should be doing, which is thinking up new ways to operate better.

If you think hard enough about it, you may be able to cite examples of proposals that got a go-ahead without a cost-benefit analysis of values, such as reducing the number of steps in a process from fourteen to three or speeding up cycle time 20 to 30 percent. Sometimes simply keeping your budget requests in line with the average in your industry is enough of an argument without having to calculate the added dollar values you will be able to deliver with the funds. Just the fact that it can be difficult to quantify some values in hard numbers may give you a sufficient excuse.

All of these rejections of taking a return-on-investment approach to budget requests are on borrowed time. Their heyday was the 1980s. By the year 2000, they will all be artifacts in the annals of management because top managers have come to a conclusion about them: They would rather have you spend your time analyzing a project's costs and benefits than be forced to spend their own time trying to make a decision without the numbers. When it comes down to your time versus top management's time, there is no way you can win.

If you keep in mind that the only reason your top managers let you borrow company money is to invest it with interest—to add to its value while it is in your hands—you will know what drives them to release their funds to you: the chance to multiply the value of the funds by putting them to work to reduce costs or gain new revenues. When you go upstairs to consult with management about their investments, remember that your counsel will never be more compelling than the value of your returns.

How much over and above each dollar you ask for will top management get back and when will they get it? If your returns speak well for you, nothing else you say will matter. If they do not, nothing else you say will matter either.

# Part I

## Making the Fit

### Changing the Way
### You Position Yourself

# 1

# Positioning Yourself
# as Partnerable

"The Borden Company is a cash machine," its chairman Romeo Ventres used to say.

If you asked him what Borden made, Ventres would say cash, not dairy products. If you asked him what Borden processed, he would say cash flows, not cheese. If you asked him what gave him a warm and furry feeling, he would say getting his investments returned at a profit, not Elsie the Cow.

Upstairs, Borden meant money. Yet downstairs, Borden meant many other things. Its plant managers saw Borden as a manufacturing machine. Its inventory managers saw Borden as a materials handling machine at the same time its R & D managers saw Borden as an invention machine and its advertising managers saw Borden as a promotion machine.

When these managers went upstairs to propose budgets, they were talking to themselves. They promised more and better products, faster information, fewer overstocks and backorders from outstocks, and more breakthrough products and blockbuster ad campaigns. In common with all chairmen, Romeo Ventres had no way to tell a blockbuster ad from a lemon. Nor could he know if faster information would lead to faster and better decisions that would generate more cash or if there would be a market for breakthrough products. All he really wanted to know was how many new dollars of profit any of these things would mean to Borden from either more revenues or fewer costs.

Without knowing how each proposal fit his objectives to make Borden a low-cost producer and a high-volume marketer, there was no way he could tell how to put his money where his objectives were. Some managers who should not have been funded came away with money, and that was bad. What was worse was that other managers who should have been funded came away empty-handed.

The next time you go upstairs, take the funder's credo with you: *Funds Follow Fit*.

Ask yourself two questions about your fit:

1. *Does my request for funds fit one of top management's key business objectives?* If it does, you can position your request in front of where funds are already flowing so you have the best chance of intercepting some of them. In order to do this, you must show how your proposal makes it likely to achieve the business objective to an even greater degree than top management has planned or faster than planned or with greater certainty.

2. *Does my request fit top management's checklist for evaluating appropriations requests?* If it does, you can reposition your request from being rejected as an added cost to being accepted as an added value that enhances corporate competitiveness. In order to do this you must transform your appropriations requests into appropriations results by selling management on the outcomes you will contribute in terms of their returns on investment and payback times.

## Putting Money in Management's Pockets

Getting funded, which means getting the budget you want when you want it, requires that you be able to prove to top management that they will be refunded from your proposal's outcomes; in other words, that they will end up in an enhanced profit position through your ability to manage an allocation of their assets so that they come back worth more than when they were put out.

This means that when you try to put your hand into top management's pockets, the first thing you must do is prove how much more money you can put back in. The amount you take out will become top management's investment in budgeting you. The amount you put back in becomes their return. The relationship between the two is the rate of return, the ROI. Top managers express it this way: For every dollar I give you, how much over and above it will I get back—a dollar and a half, two and a half dollars, five or ten dollars? When will I get it? How sure can I be?

These are the three horsemen of funding: *how much, how soon,* and *how sure.* How you score on at least two of them determines which pile your proposal goes into when top management makes their selection-by-triage:

*Pile 1:* Must fund.
*Pile 2:* May or may not fund.
*Pile 3:* No way will we fund.

Your top managers have the same problem you do: how to control costs yet still manage a world-class operation. You have the problem for your unit or division or department or business function or process. They have the problem for the company as a whole. Both of you look everywhere for every way to improve productivity and quality, to contribute as little cost as possible, and to maximize your contribution to revenues. The only difference is that they have every manager competing for their funds. The best chance of getting the funds you ask for in the shortest approval time is to close the culture gap between top management and you. If you go around thinking "How can I *improve our operations?*" you will have no way to fit in with top management's preoccupation with how your operation can *improve their profits.*

The gap between these two mind-sets is the difference between turning on management's approval or being turned down. Optimizing your own performance ends up in pile 2 or 3. Helping top management maximize profits gets you into pile 1.

Your funds requests get approval when you can prove that their contribution to corporate profits meets two criteria:

1. The company will make money on them.
2. You will make more money for the company as their investor than another manager.

This is known as the "Business Case" strategy for getting funded. It is a strategy to integrate the technical culture of running an operation with the financial culture of running a business. Making the case for a business reason for funds is the bridge between managers who need money and top managers who need the money their managers can make on the money they lend them. When the culture gap between mid-level and top managers remains unbridged, miscommunication and misunderstanding result in missed opportunities to grow businesses or right-size them or to acquire or divest technologies, products, processes, and markets.

Managing investments is top management's job. They allocate investment funds based on expected returns—expectation that is expressed as "What do I get back and when do I get it?" Unless you can make a case for your request for funds that responds to top management's request for a preview of the results, you risk going unfunded or underfunded—of coming downstairs with a diminished return on your own investment in preparing and presenting your budget.

## Getting up Front in the Long Line of Requests

As far as top management is concerned, all proposals to contribute improved profits to key business objectives are grey. It makes no difference which ones get funded; only their results count. It is to management's advantage to encourage open competition for its funds. Out of competition, the belief is that the best investment opportunities will survive—so will the best investors.

Management's attitude toward funding is to act in the manner of an auctioneer: Here are the funds; what am I bid in return? Top managers think less about funding an operation than funding a specific investor—an individual "money manager." Lending money is a good-faith act. Faith is placed in people, not projects. It is the result of a combination of soul-searching and record-searching:

- Can this man or woman deliver? What does the track record say? What does my gut feeling tell me? Are they the same?
- Is the project too big for the manager? Is its time frame too tight? Has he or she ever ridden a horse like this before? Will I end up at the finish line with a riderless horse (a thrown manager) or a horseless rider (a lost horse)?

- How deeply committed is the manager to the project? (Is this a labor of love that will consume him or her seven days a week, or is it just another job? Is there enough fire in the belly to be willing to die to get the profits on the bottom line?
- Is this someone who will call for help if trouble comes, or will he or she try to be heroic and put out fires all alone until they blaze out of control? Is this an egocentric manager or someone centered on the greater good?
- If I were down to my last dollar, is this the person I would choose to invest it with in an all-or-nothing shootout?

Top managers have affection for scramblers—middle managers who scratch and scrounge for funds by coming up with good deals for the use of management's money. A reputation as a funds fighter may not get you any more money all by itself, but it will get you many more opportunities to propose. The question that goes through top management's thought-process when they look up and see you standing on their doorstep, "What does he want?" will have a reflexive answer: "He wants to make another one of his contributions to improving our profits."

The more you focus on how good you are as a manager of your operation, the less you will be able to see yourself from top management's perspective. Before your top managers fund you, they want you to prove how good you are as a manager of their money. Are you a blue-chip investment? Is a dollar under your management a better investment than the same dollar under someone else's management? How do you compare on muchness—the amount you produce; on soonness—the time it takes you to produce; and on sureness—the certainty that you can produce the amount you propose within the time you propose to produce it?

You come home with the money when you fit into the flow of funds, which is always in the direction of business objectives. That is half the battle. The other half is how management pays off the next time around. What did you do with their money? Did their investment get paid back with interest? Was the interest paid on time? This is top management's way of reminding you that there is no free lunch. What you can take out is always in proportion to what your track record says you normally put back in and what your current proposal says you are most likely to put in this time.

When the last-time numbers are bad, or when they show a declining trend over time, there may be no next time.

As far as top management is concerned, running your operation means running its numbers. If you run a cost center, running the numbers means running down your current costs by reducing or eliminating them and avoiding unnecessary future costs. If you run a revenue or profit center, running the numbers means running up the amount of money you make or running up the speed with which you make it.

If you run an R & D laboratory as a technician, you will see your job as coming up with innovative products. But if it costs you more than the products earn when they get to market, or if they get to a market too late to cream its profits, or if they incur high costs of repair or replacement under warranty, you are not running your operation as a business manager. It will show up when you go for funding.

If you run a manufacturing plant as an engineer, you will see your job as producing customer-satisfying products. But if your downtime and your rework rates are high while your order-to-shipment cycle time is also high, you are not running your operation as a business manager. It will show up when you go for funding.

If you run information systems as a computer scientist, you will see your job as making data accessible across the enterprise, permitting concurrent product design and development to go on in several places in the world at the same time, and automating the sales force. But if your systems fail to get product to market faster or measurably improve productivity, you are not running your operation as a business manager. It will show up when you go for funding.

When you run your operation to return top management's investments at a significant multiple, you become a preferred candidate for funds. It signals that you understand top management's unspoken way of regarding anyone who comes before them asking for funds:

> You have to understand that there is a long line of requests for capital. All substantial requests are supported

by extensive homework on the economic performance benefits of each project. If you are going to come up here and compete for the same dollars, you are going to have to present us with these kinds of results data so that we can support making an investment in your project and bump someone else out of line in your favor. Otherwise you're going to be left standing around with a long face and short funds.

Are you a major contributor to cost reduction, either in your own operation or elsewhere in the organization? This shows that you are a good money manager. Are you a major contributor to increased sales revenues or to reducing the costs of current revenues? This shows that you are a good money manager. Nothing else you manage means as much as your skill in managing money. You may think that you manage people or inventory or receivables collections; your title may call you a product development manager or a manufacturing manager or a manager of information systems. No matter; from where top management sits, you are an *asset manager.*

Every asset you manage is a cost. Your job is to make more money on it than its cost or cut back on its cost to the point where you can make it pay off. When you propose additional assets, the same job description applies. Its message is that every new cost you take on must pay for itself and then show a profit from the new revenues it contributes to or establish a new lower cost base for your operation.

By positioning yourself as a money manager, what if you can get just one additional appropriations request funded this year? What if you can get funding faster by only one percent less time? How many more dollars will that give you to make your operation more competitive this year?

## Acquiring an Upstairs Mind-Set

Top managers look to their operating managers to buy into the strategic business vision of the company and to know how they can maximize their contribution to it—in other words, to know how their contribution fits into company-wide objectives and to take ownership of it.

At the top, there are broadband enterprise goals. Function-specific goals are narrowband: contribute this much less cost to the enterprise or this much more revenue, or the same revenue at this much less cost. In order to meet your function goals, top management gives you the power to act like a general manager. If you manage R & D, you are likely empowered to be a general manager of a quasiautonomous research and development organization.* That hat is all right for you to wear downstairs. But when you go upstairs for funds, you are expected to wear a hat that integrates your function with management's strategic business vision. What you are doing for R & D is no longer the issue. Management wants to know what R&D is doing for them.

If you manage information technology (IT), you are empowered to be a general manager of a quasiautonomous technology organization. Upstairs your hat must make you out to be an integrator of corporate systems and a reengineer of corporate processes so you can help implement the vision of the enterprise.

Similarly, if you manage manufacturing, you are empowered to be a general manager of a quasiautonomous organization that stamps or punches or mills or melts and smelts. Upstairs, your hat must make you out to be a low-cost, high-quality, just-in-time, best-of-breed insource that performs just as cost-effectively as an outsource.

Whether or not you are dressed for success when you go upstairs for funds depends on which hat you wear. If you present the standard request for appropriations, you position yourself in top management's eyes as a functionary whose objectives are operational and not strategic. But if you wear your enterprise hat, you link yourself to the corporate business strategy with a business case—not an operating case—that positions your contribution to the overall objectives of the organization. It is your fit that will earn funds far more than your function.

No single argument can position you with top management more compellingly than the business case you present for funds.

*To learn more about managing under empowerment, see my book *Manage Like You Own It* (New York: AMACOM, 1994).

Top managers take money very seriously. After all, they run a cash machine. They know to the dollar how much they have had to gross in order to end up with the net amount they took to the bank and that you want a piece of. They know how much each dollar costs them if they borrow. When you come to them to improve your operation, their interest is the improvement it can make in their profits.

Improvement has its own meaning at the top. Downstairs, you talk continuous business process improvement. Top management talks continuous earnings improvement and continuous improvement in cost control. You talk productivity management, but top management hears the added costs to achieve it and the lack of certainty in quantifying its contributions. The same miscommunication occurs when you talk quality and top management hears only the added costs of quality. Will any savings result? Will new revenues be gained? If you are unable to offset your costs by creating counterbalancing values, you are running a "roach motel" for funds: Management's money goes in, but nothing comes out.

Never let it be said of your operation what is frequently said of IT, of flexible manufacturing systems, and—deservedly so—of most sales training: "After a generation of impressive investment, there is little evidence to support improvements in productivity—or any other measure of business performance."

If your function management is at risk of becoming synonymous with "roach motel" management, you need to close the mind-set gap with your managers at the top. Each day when you open up shop, get reacquainted with your variable costs. Ask yourself how you can maximize their contribution to profits. Every pound or yard or gallon of materials you order or store or use up or waste adds a variable cost to the deadweight of your fixed assets. So does every man-hour of labor. Every hour of downtime turns good money into bad. Every workstation is a cost when it sits idle or an even greater cost when unproductive work flows through it. Each minute of its cycle time adds more cost. You, of course, are the greatest cost. How does it all contribute to the business of making money?

How much money do you make on every dollar invested in your operation? By how much do you reduce the cost of making money for every dollar invested? Can the same investment be managed better to produce an even greater return? If not, how are you going to get funded when the hurdle for funding is to be a supplier of more money than you apply for?

## Condensing the Funding Cycle

Your challenge to position yourself in line with management's strategic business vision is to learn to stop asking for funds to improve your operation and start providing refunds that can improve top management's competitiveness.

This new position requires you to relinquish the operating manager's fixation on performance benefits and translate them into financial benefits. The financial benefits of performance improvement constitute the heart and soul of approvable budget requests.

The funding cycle is an insider's selling process. Mid-level managers sell returns. Top management buys them, paying for them by making investments with their middle managers. The process is an internal application of Consultative Selling℠,* which can help you in five ways to condense the funding cycle:

1. You propose to create new values instead of spending past values.
2. You propose investment opportunities instead of costs.
3. You propose returns on management's investments instead of trying to justify their costs.
4. You propose in the form and content of business cases that top management reflexively understands instead of operating budgets that you have to go along with to explain.
5. You propose that top management compete more cost-effectively instead of proposing competitively against your fellow managers.

The internal application of Consultative Selling is top management's strategy of choice when you sell upstairs. It is based on transforming appropriations requests into business cases called

---

*Consultative Selling is a registered trademark of Mack Hanan. To learn more about its strategies, see my book *Consultative Selling℠*, Fourth Edition (New York: AMACOM, 1991).

Profit Improvement Proposals™ (PIPs™).* A PIP is a bird's-eye view of the three things that top managers want to know: *how much* added value will be returned for each dollar funded, *how soon* it will be returned, and *how sure* they can be that the return will be realized.

Because Consultative Selling sells money, and not its intermediary contributions such as staff reallocations or performance improvement, it condenses your sales cycle for getting funded. No longer can top management trade off time to avoid the cost of funding you. The time value of money in a consultative proposal tells management how much cash flow they are losing out on while they make up their minds. Time becomes your salesman. Delay works against management because it incurs opportunity cost. Signing off on your proposal becomes the way to start a flow of new cash. The constant pressure at the top to improve profits is management's incentive to close your profit-improvement proposals. Each day's debate postpones payback and moves the onset of management's return on its investment at least twenty-four hours into the future. Every postponed dollar will be worth less when it is received than it is worth today. In effect, your proposal is transformed into a depreciating asset rather than an appreciating one.

As far as top management is concerned, the standards of performance that merit funding you can be summed up as follows:

- You are performing according to your operating standards when you manage continuous improvement in the cost-effectiveness of your operation.
- You are performing according to your standards of business management when you manage continuous improvement of your operation's contributions to company profits. This requires its costs to be continually reduced, its contributions to revenue and earnings to be continually increased, or—in the case of a profit center—both.

*Profit Improvement Proposal and its acronym PIP are registered trademarks of Mack Hanan. If you manage an operation in an educational institution; a government agency, bureau, or department; or any other nonprofit or not-for-profit organization, substitute Cost-Reduction Proposal or Revenue-Improvement Proposal for Profit Improvement Proposal and base your proposals on reduced costs or increased revenues instead of contributions to profits.

Return on investment is the standard measurement tool that top managers use to evaluate your performance as a business manager. It compares how much they give you with how much you give them back: your bang for their bucks.

In order to carry out your business mission, you will have to figure out what kind of business you are supporting or supplying with your operating capabilities. If the business gets along on low unit margins and makes its money on volume generated by high turnover, look to add value to its ROI through improved order entry, shipping, and receivables collection. If the business has a relatively low turnover and makes its money on high unit margins, look to add value to its ROI through speeding up the cycle time of new product development and implementing new distribution systems.

- If you manage a service function like information technology (IT) or human resources (HR) and you want to upgrade your own operation, target the current contribution to your total costs being made by one of your operation's critical work flows or its cycle time and propose to reduce them. If you want to upgrade someone else's operation like manufacturing or inventory management, or help achieve a corporate objective like faster time-to-market or lower cost of quality, target a critical work flow and its cycle times and propose to reduce its costs or increase its ability to realize added revenues.

- If you manage a cost center like R & D, manufacturing, or sales and marketing, target a current contribution to your total costs being made by one of your operation's critical work flows and propose to reduce it or propose an increased contribution to revenues by speeding up development cycles, time-to-market cycles, or sales cycles. In both cases, you must know two things: (1) the current costs you propose to reduce or the current revenues you propose to increase; and (2) the incremental values you propose—the negative values you can subtract from current costs in order to reduce them and the positive values you can add to current revenues and earnings in order to increase them.

Figure 1-1 shows the typical cycle of proposing for funds. It can be summarized in six words: *middle management proposes, top*

**Figure 1-1.** The funding cycle.

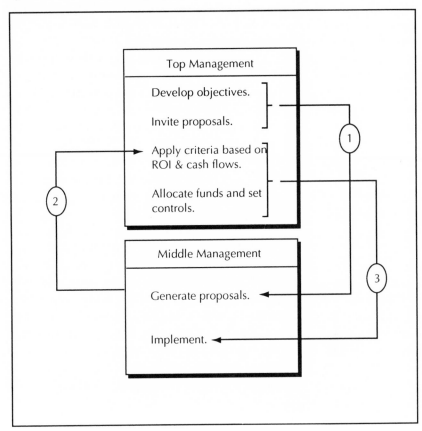

*management disposes.* Top management's role is to develop objectives for the business. Once they set direction, they invite middle managers to propose how to help them get there:

- How their line-of-business profit-center managers can generate the required revenues and earnings at controlled levels of cost
- How their business-function cost-center managers can support the business lines with cost-effective productivity at required levels of quality

In Figure 1-1, vector #1 represents the invitations to propose for funds that top management sends downstairs. Middle management's responses are shown by vector #2, along which their proposals flow upstairs. When top management approves, funds get allocated, controls are set, and implementation starts along vector #3.

## Becoming Top Management's Partner in Profit Improvement

The objective of using Consultative Selling strategies to sell upstairs is to enable you to become a profit partner of top management. A profit partnership at the top opens up to you as soon as you ally your objectives in requesting funds with management's objectives in allocating them. Common objectives are the first principle of partnering. They are the essence of a win-win relationship.

In partnering upstairs, you are the consultant partner and top managers are your client partners. Without their funds, you cannot operate. But without your ability to grow their funds by investing them in profit-improvement projects, top management cannot manage their cash machine. Unless the business makes money, and then makes more money on the money it makes, the people at the top are mismanaging it.

By calculating what you can do with their money to grow it, your budget requests advise management on how to put it to the best use. This is your consultant role. It is a continuous role, since management needs continuous profit improvement to stay competitive. This means that you are expected to place fundable investment opportunities before management in an uninterrupted sequence, not just quarterly or semiannually or annually. Downtime in proposing fundable projects is mutually unaffordable to you and to them, as are unimplementable projects that turn out to be scrap, or projects that must be recalled partway through to completion or turned over to an outsourcer.

High productivity in the generation of profit-improvement proposals is key to partnering. So is the quality of each proposal, since money assets that turn out to be unrecoverable, or that do not earn their proposed return, cannot easily—or perhaps ever—be replaced.

Top management looks to you for an unending supply of "what ifs," proposed projects to improve your operation's contribution to profits: a challenge like "What if we can return $1.5 million for every $1 million invested by the end of twenty-four months, with payback occurring within year one?"

As a consultant you are management's "What if?" partner. Management, in turn, is your "How?" partner, wanting to know how you plan to improve your contributions to profits once you prove that your proposals are significant enough and timely enough—that is, they contain sufficient muchness and soonness—to make management comfortable to go further. From that point on, everything focuses on minimizing foreseeable risk so that sureness can be maximized.

Management expects of you a paradoxical mixture of financial opportunities in formulating fundable proposals and financial conservatism in preserving assets and in returning borrowed funds with interest by their due dates. Fiscal conservatism makes you a comfortable partner. Opportunistic project formulation makes you a productive one.

As with all partners, you will be known by the continuity of value you add to the partnership. You are always at risk to answer "What have you done for me lately?" because there is no end to management's uses for money. Accordingly, there can be no end to your capability as a source of supply for management's cash machine.

# 2

# Adding Value
# Instead of Cost

Business values exist in the form of quantified dollar values. This is the only form that business values come in. Dollars exist in the form of 100 cents each. This is the only form that dollars come in. There is no such thing as "more dollars" or "a lot of dollars," just as there is no such amount of time called "soon."

Values have meaning only when they are expressed in hard numbers, which are dollar values that are readily quantifiable. Dollars saved by reducing or eliminating a cost are hard dollars. They can drop one-for-one to the bottom line. Other values are softer, like dollars that may or may not be earned by potential new sales. No one can be sure of the eventual value of trying to increase revenue dollars. The sales may or may not be there. But the value of dollars saved by reducing costs is much easier to quantify.

Soft values command a low level of confidence because they are unquantifiable. They have a perceived value, and most managers may agree that they have some worth, but no one can agree on exactly how much value will accrue or how soon. Soft values lack sureness. As a result, they cannot compel investment.

Improved operating flexibility is a soft value. So is faster responsiveness to changing market needs. Until they can be converted to hard-number outcomes in the form of dollarized reduced costs or sales revenues based on proven market demand, they are unbudgetable.

Customer satisfaction is another soft value. The value added by a proposal to improve customer satisfaction is unquantifiable unless you can document the contribution of each percentage point of increased satisfaction to each dollar of increased sales revenue or reduced costs. Similarly, the value added by a proposal to improve productivity is unquantifiable unless you can document the contribution of each percentage point of reduced labor costs to each dollar of increased sales revenues or reduced costs: Either output per worker must go up or labor intensity must be reduced by reallocation or right-sizing.

If you go for funds to improve productivity without hard values, you must be prepared to deal with questions like these from the top:

- How much will productivity be increased? If it is not enough to permit the labor force to be rationalized, why bother?
- How much more work will be produced? If it cannot be sold because there is no demand for it, or if it cannot be sold at high margins because it consists of commodity products, why bother?
- How much more sales revenue will be earned? If it does not reflect an acceptable revenue-to-investment ratio, why bother?

Figure 2-1 shows the comparative measurability of common operating values. You will find productivity in the right-hand column of softer values that are hard to quantify. Values in the left-hand column are more readily measurable in hard numbers and are, for that reason, a good deal more proposable.

## Basing Budgets on Value

Creating value through the improvement of management's profits and measuring the value you create are the Siamese twins of getting funded. Unless you measure the financial improvements your projects contribute, you will not know your values; unless you know your values, you will not be able to demonstrate consistently predictable performance; without provable consistency in "making plan," you will have no track record to testify to your accountability as a money manager.

There are two rules for ensuring accountability:

**Figure 2-1.** Comparative value measurability.

| Readily Measurable Values | Hard-to-Measure Values |
|---|---|
| Meantime between new product introductions | Time saved |
| | Quality improved |
| Time and cost of product development cycle | Productivity gained |
| | Capability enhanced |
| Forecast accuracy compared to actual results | Motivation increased |
| Inventory costs | Communication speeded |
| Process scheduling accuracy compared to actual results | Information learned |
| | Satisfaction elevated |
| Speed of order entry | |
| Meantime between billings and collections | |
| Receivables outstanding | |
| Reject and scrap rates | |
| Downtime rates | |
| Meantime between downtimes | |
| Product movement from warehouses | |
| Product movement at retail | |

1. Measure the values you propose.
2. Propose only measurable values.

If you go valueless before top management with an unquantified appropriations request, you will be representing yourself as a value-subtractor instead of a value-adder—in other words, as a cost, which is an expenditure, without a predicted return. Where are your offsetting cash flows? Management will ask. If you have no answer, it means that your budget is a price without redemption—a pig in a poke. As with all prices, top management will grind you down.

Getting ground down on your budget's price tag means debating with management on the merits of what you are asking for. Why do you need so much money? Why for these things? Why now? When you get into debating the merits, you are fighting for leftovers. On the other hand, when you sell on value, top management will ask you value-based questions. Why can't you contribute more? Why can't you contribute it sooner? What resources do you need in order to contribute more and contribute it sooner?

Unknown value is valueless. You cannot use it to obtain funds. Unquantified narrative value is equally valueless. You cannot get something called "money" simply by proposing something called "value." Without putting a number on your value, management cannot put a number on the most cost-effective investment. One number is worth a thousand words.

Top managers are reluctant guessers. If you leave it to top managers to guess your contributions of value, they will play it safe by underestimating your most likely values and overestimating your most likely costs. This follows management's rule for resolving doubt: Underestimate revenues and overestimate their costs. Once your value becomes downsized in management's perception, your funds will shrink to fit it.

## Knowing Your Values

Top management's preferred funding model is performance-based budgeting, which funds you for the value of your proposed outcome rather than for the costs of achieving it.

Top managers buy only one thing: value in the form of returns on their investments. Since management is in no other market than the market for value, there is nothing else you can sell them. If you are an IT manager, what does automated materials handling mean to them or, for that matter, same-day order fulfillment or flexible manufacturing? If you make a traditional cost-based proposal for funds, you may budget automating the materials handling function as a $10 million cost. How can management tell if this is or is not a good deal unless you propose the incremental profits that will flow in return? If the return value turns out to be $15 million, every dollar that management puts into automated materials handling will yield $1.50. Top management relates to that in this manner: Automated materials handling is a way for us to make 50 cents on a dollar. Unless management has a better offer on the table for investing its supply of dollars, automated materials handling will be a fundable proposition if the only alternative is to incur opportunity cost.

Basing your budgets on the value you can contribute to financial performance forces you to think like top management. If you want funds to improve your operation's productivity, think like management and propose the added values of greater sales volume, or greater market share, or a greater number of orders filled and billed the same day they are received. If you want funds to improve your operation's quality, think like management and propose the added values of higher margins, fewer rejects, less scrap, or reduced materials costs.

## Controlling Your Values

Once you see your number-one job as helping your top managers run their business more competitively—which is already the way your top managers see your job—you will be incented to take control of your values. Your contribution to management's cash flows becomes your "product," the ultimate outcome of running your operation. Whether you make your contribution through the way you manage inventory, or develop new products, or get orders out the door, or set up local area networks is irrelevant. The only thing that matters is the contribution to cash flow that nets out.

Your ability to control the consistent delivery of your value is your single greatest test as a manager. Value control requires diligence. You must keep an eye on quality and the costs of quality. Neither is a value in itself but both contribute to value. You must keep an eye on productivity and the costs of productivity. Neither is a value in itself but both contribute to value. You must keep an eye on the interaction between quality and productivity. Too much emphasis on either can counteract the value contributed by the other.

Your value makes you partnerable upstairs. But only if you control your value so that you can be accepted as a reliable provider will you be partnered—not just considered as a candidate for funds, but funded. If management comes to believe that your consistency as a value-adder is no longer predictable, your partnership will become marginal. Businesses run on predictability. This is why proposed improvements that approach the six-sigma level of 99.9997 perfection are often the enemy of incremental improvements that are "good enough" to maintain competitive advantage and, at the same time, do not bet the business or break the bank.

### Controlling Value Through the Development Cycle

"Good enough" means just what it says: funding enough investment for continuous improvement to sustain enough competitive advantage in customer satisfaction to dominate a market. Investments over and above the good-enough level can add more to cost than to value. The "good enoughness" curve shown in Figure 2-2 relates the Pareto principle of the 80-20 rule to product development.

**Figure 2-2.** The "good enoughness" curve.

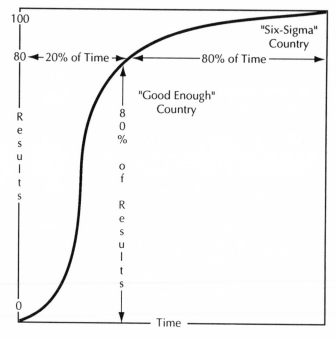

As the figure shows, the first 20 percent of an investment generally yields up to 80 percent of the eventual benefits. The remaining 80 percent of investment yields only grudging shares of the remaining potential benefits. Whenever the point of "good enoughness" is reached, further investment should be allocated somewhere else.

This is why investment should never be maximized, only optimized to produce value that is good enough. A rule to remember at the start of each investment cycle is to ask not how much investment you need for technical superiority, but how little you need to ensure continuing competitive advantage through questions like these:

- How little incremental quality do I have to build into my product?
- How little incremental improvement in time-to-market do I have to build into my order entry?
- How little incremental reduction in scrap do I have to build into my manufacturing?
- How little incremental market segmentation do I have to build into my advertising?

By asking how little rather than how much, and by thinking in increments instead of giant steps, you can avoid creating operating costs that make no proportional contribution to the creation of value. You will have achieved the essence of value control, which is knowing the difference between what can be done technically and what will maximize cost-effectiveness—in short, the difference between what is nice and what is necessary.

### Controlling Value Through the Life Cycle

Value-adding priorities change throughout the life cycle of a product or service, an operating process, or a business.

Figure 2-3 shows the classic four-stage model of a business life cycle, beginning with its startup, moving into market entry, growth, and finally becoming mature. Your opportunities to add value are specific to each stage of the cycle, as the following guidelines show:

**Figure 2-3.** Business life cycle.

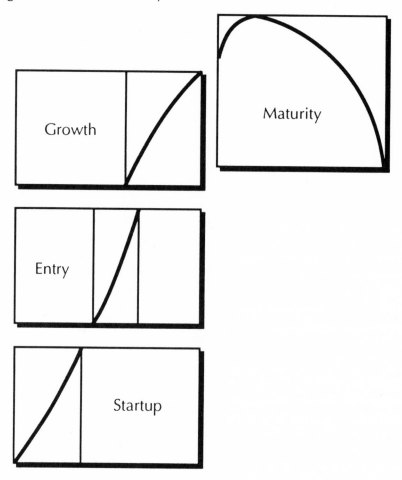

*Value-Adding Opportunities for Startup Ventures*

- Make market entry on time or earlier or less expensively.
- Ensure product reliability to avoid repairs under warranty or recall.
- Avoid unnecessary fixed costs.
- Set up inventory to prevent backordering or overstocking.

### Value-Adding Opportunities for Entry

- Standardize volume operations.
- Ensure order-fulfillment and shipments.
- Organize billing and collection.
- Accelerate breakeven.

### Value-Adding Opportunities in Growth

- Maximize sales volume.
- Generate family of products.
- Test next entry.
- Institute total quality management.
- Control variable costs.
- Ensure continuity of cash flow.

### Value-Adding Opportunities in Maturity

- Control variable costs.
- Increase market share.
- Differentiate products and services.
- Increase productivity.
- Decrease cost of sales.

Your profit-improvement projects throughout the life cycle should adhere to these guidelines to make sure that each individual proposal is on target with business strategy. Generally speaking, you can count on management's agreement with four initiatives: to take startup operations to market as fast as possible, to move quickly from market entry to growth, to speed up growth so that profits can be maximized in the shortest time, and to perpetuate growth as long as possible into maturity in order to postpone decline.

## Adding Value by Internal Services

Information technology, human resources, and sales training and management development are business functions whose managers must budget for the needs of other managers who are their internal constituents, as well as for their own needs. Internal services are valued—and therefore budgeted—according to how much they help the company's line managers and function managers in R & D, manufacturing, sales, and marketing to improve their contributions to corporate profits. The ability of an internal-service managers to act as a value-adder depends on knowing where constituents need revenue increases or cost reductions and being able to propose profit-improvement projects to help realize them. In this way, IT, HR, and sales training managers can help their internal customers fit into company-wide business strategy.

Fitting in with business strategy means getting in front of top management's flow of funds allocated to core capabilities—the core businesses and critical-to-success operations whose processes serve the core businesses. When management says that it must be in this market or that, or this or that competency is vital to competitiveness, it is setting business strategy. In other words, it is telling you where to look for leads to propose profit-improvement projects that have a high probability of getting funded.

When top management publishes its "must list" of the businesses it says in each year's annual report and 10K that it must be in, and the core competencies it must own in order to serve them, you are being given your leads to target for profit projects. You will find proposable leads to help generate incremental revenues and to help reduce costs in three sets of performance indicators for each line of business:

- Financial performance
- Operating ratio performance
- Working capital performance

### Key Financial Performance Indicators

You can find leads to propose profit-improvement projects by looking at four indicators of the financial performance for a line of business.

1. *Total revenues.* Can they be raised by a project you can propose? Total revenues are the sum of all receipts from sales. You can propose improving their contribution to profits if you can speed

up time to market, increase the turnover rate of the product development cycle, improve forecasting, or reduce inventory of slow-moving items while reducing stockouts of items in high demand, improving and enlarging distribution, or accelerating billings and collections.

2. *Total operating income.* Can it be raised by a project you can propose? Total operating income is pretax net revenues—the result of subtracting total operating expenses from gross profits (gross margin). You can propose improving its contribution to profits if you can reallocate funds to sales and away from operating expenses.

3. *Total operating expenses.* Can they be lowered by a project you can propose? Total operating expenses are the sum of the cost of sales plus general and administrative (G & A) plus research and development (R & D). You can propose improving their contribution to profits if you can take costs out of any of them.

4. *Cost of goods sold.* Can it be lowered by a project you can propose? You can propose improving its contribution to profits if you can improve sales-force productivity, reduce the sales cycle, improve or increase distribution, open up new markets, or reengineer sales strategy.

### Key Operating Ratio Performance Indicators

You can find leads to propose profit-improvement projects by looking at four indicators of the operating ratio performance for a line of business.

1. *Gross profit* (gross margin). Can it be raised by a project you can propose? Gross profit is the ratio of total revenues to the cost of goods sold. You can propose improving its contribution to profits if you can increase sales volume and expand share of market, speed up the sales cycle, improve or increase distribution, increase the turnover rate of the product-development cycle, or reduce manufacturing costs.

2. *Net profit.* Can it be raised by a project you can propose? Net profit is total net earnings—the ratio of after-tax net income to net sales. It shows the percentage of each sales dollar that is re-

tained after taxes. You can propose improving its contribution to profits if you can increase margins, reduce cost of sales, or reallocate the sales mix to favor more high-margin products and services.

3. *Productivity.* Can it be raised by a project you can propose? Productivity is the ratio of sales revenues to the number of people required to generate them. You can propose improving its contribution to profits if you can reduce labor content, increase automation, improve workforce training, or implement pay-for-performance compensation schedules.

4. *Selling efficiency.* Can it be raised by a project you can propose? Selling efficiency is composed of five ratios based on sales revenues. You can propose improving its contribution to profits if you can improve any one of them:

- Cost of sales : sales revenues
- Finished goods inventory : sales revenues
- Order backlog : sales revenues
- Same-day order fulfillment : sales revenues
- Accounts receivable : sales revenues

### Working Capital Performance Indicators

You can find leads to propose profit-improvement projects by looking at two indicators of the working capital performance for a line of business.

1. *Inventory turnover.* Can it be increased by a project you can propose? Inventory turnover is the ratio of annual net sales to end-of-year inventory of finished goods. You can propose improving its contribution to profits if you can reduce inventory by making it turn faster. Any decrease in inventory automatically increases cash.

2. *Accounts receivable turnover.* Can it be increased by a project you can propose? Accounts receivable turnover is the ratio of net sales revenues to the average dollar value of receivables outstanding. You can propose improving its contribution to profits if you can reduce receivables by collecting them faster. Any decrease in receivables automatically increases cash.

# Proposing at the "Power of One"

When you propose financial benefits from investing in your operations, you do not have to go gangbusters to be a compelling money manager. A little financial improvement goes a long way. Always start your proposal process at the smallest whole-number rate of improvement: the number one. Get a sense of its power. If it is "good enough," you can become a continuous improver of your operation's contributions to profits at the lowest level of risk.

One percent may not seem like much. But a one percent reduction in the cost of quality for a $6 billion business yields $60 million in savings that come from reduced cost of goods sold, lower sales and administrative costs, and control over new-product–development costs. A one penny reduction in an airline's cost of flying each seat-mile comes to an additional $600 million a year in added revenues. A one-minute reduction in the time an airplane stays on the ground each flight can be worth $45 million in revenues per year.

There is improved value everywhere at the one percent level. In many manufacturing businesses, the cost of quality can be 35 percent of sales. What if you can reduce it to 34 percent? In many service businesses, the cost of quality can be as much as 70 percent of sales. What if you can reduce it to 69 percent? How many new dollars of improved profits will each one percent improvement contribute?

The "power of one" can make contributions millions of times over in the form of one more product sold every day, one more percentage point added to current revenues or profits every week, or one less day every quarter required to collect accounts receivable. Applying the "power of one" also appeals to top-level comfort. Management is comfortable with the idea that someone in charge of a typical operation can deal with increments of one without incurring undue costs and inefficiencies, whose disruptions could nullify their gains. Furthermore, the number one has the power of credibility. On its face, it appears doable.

If you are a manufacturing manager and you can eliminate one part from a major product, you can free yourself from ten contributions to cost. You will no longer have to:

- Design it.
- Assign a part number to it.
- Inventory it.
- Shelve it.
- Inspect it.
- Assemble it.
- Repair it.
- Package it.
- Handle it.
- Deliver it.

If you are a sales and marketing manager, can you enlarge a market opportunity by a factor of one? If you can start new mothers using baby foods one month sooner, when their babies are five instead of six months old, you can open up millions of dollars' worth of incremental annual sales.

Figures 2-4 and 2-5 show general opportunities to apply the "power of one" to revenue expansion and cost reduction.

One hour saved each day or one dollar of profit gained with each sale can make significant contributions. A one-day reduction

**Figure 2-4.** Revenue-expansion opportunities.

1. Add operational flexibility.
2. Add manufacturing or processing quality.
3. Add volume.
4. Improve effectiveness of sales department.
5. Introduce new sizes, shapes, or materials or new and improved products.
6. Reduce customer returns.
7. Apply creative sales promotion strategies.
8. Speed up production and distribution.
9. Reduce or eliminate unprofitable products, customers, warehouses, or territories.
10. Improve market position.
11. Add brand name value.
12. Add customer benefits.
13. Extend product life.
14. Expand into new markets.
15. Increase distribution.

**Figure 2-5.** Cost-reduction opportunities.

*From Cutting Purchase Costs*
1. Reduce number of types of articles in stock.
2. Standardize preferred items.
3. Shop market for optimal supplier quality, delivery, and cost.
4. Centralize negotiations for major items.
5. Plan ahead to reduce rush procurement.
6. Subject bids and contracts to periodic review.
7. Conduct make-or-buy studies.
8. Speed up invoice processing to avoid discount losses.
9. Inspect incoming shipments to minimize damage from defects.
10. Speed up disposal of slow-moving inventories.
11. Establish most economical production or ordering quantities.
12. Shift burden of carrying inventories to suppliers.

*From Cutting Production Costs*
1. Reduce number of operations.
2. Reduce cost of one or more operations.
3. Combine two or more operations.
4. Automate operations.
5. Reduce labor.
6. Improve production scheduling.
7. Reduce operating time to speed up production.
8. Reduce insurance costs.
9. Reduce materials consumption.
10. Recycle materials.
11. Substitute less expensive materials or otherwise reformulate product.
12. Reduce raw materials inventory.
13. Reduce parts inventory.
14. Improve controls.
15. Simplify product and package design.
16. Dedicate an entire production line to one product or customer.

*From Cutting Production Downtime*
1. Standardize preferred items.
2. Shop market for optimal supplier quality, delivery, and cost.
3. Plan ahead to reduce rush procurement.
4. Improve plant delivery system.
5. Inspect incoming shipments to minimize damage from defects.
6. Install preventive maintenance program.
7. Improve personnel training.

*(continues)*

**Figure 2-5.** (continued)

8. Improve process analysis.
9. Establish most economical production or ordering points.
10. Correlate forecasting between marketing and production.

*From Cutting Freight Costs*
1. Centralize negotiations for freight haulage.
2. Plan ahead to reduce rush procurement.
3. Prescribe preferred routing.
4. Stage incoming shipments to reduce overtime.
5. Reduce intraplant inventory transfers.
6. Utilize trucks more efficiently, or buy trucks instead of renting.
7. Relocate warehouses.
8. Reformulate product or packaging to lighten shipping weights.
9. Reduce handling costs.
10. Reduce insurance costs.

*From Cutting Administrative Overhead*
1. Reduce number of types of articles in stock.
2. Standardize preferred items.
3. Plan ahead to reduce rush procurement.
4. Combine related items on purchase orders.
5. Establish most economical production or ordering points.
6. Shift burden of carrying inventories to suppliers.
7. Control additions of new articles to stock.
8. Take inventory cycle counts when stocks are low.
9. Combine two or more operations.
10. Decrease labor force.

*From Maximizing Working Capital*
1. Reduce number of types of articles in stock.
2. Shop market for optimal supplier quality, delivery, and cost.
3. Speed up disposal of slow-moving inventories.
4. Establish most economical production or ordering points.
5. Shift burden of carrying inventories to supplier.
6. Control additions of new articles to stock.
7. Correlate forecasting data between marketing and production.
8. Make secured short-term loans of excess cash.
9. Use large-supplier's credit department to obtain optimal bank interest rates.
10. Speed up production.
11. Increase process efficiency to decrease scrap and damaged or unacceptable work.
12. Combine two or more operations.

in the length of a sales cycle, order-fulfillment cycle, or design cycle can bring in dollars that are otherwise impossible to generate at comparable cost-effectiveness. So can adding the equivalent of one additional hour of productive output to each sales cycle or just one more cent to margins on each sale or one more percent to market share.

It is a good idea to get into the habit of periodically asking two questions of your operation:

1. Where can we contribute at the one percent level to management's cost containment objectives?
2. Where can we contribute at the one percent level to management's revenue objectives?

The first thing to do is to clean up your own operation at the "power of one." Concentrate on getting rid of reducible and avoidable costs. Focus on realizing revenue opportunities that you may be leaving on the table.

Keep challenging yourself to get the best value. Will it come from eliminating or downsizing one of the 80 percent–type processes in your operation that does not add much value? Or will it come from focusing on one of the 20 percent–type processes that is crucial to your functionality because it is one of the highest value-adders?

If you provide an internal service, you should be out in the halls selling every day, in ways like these:

▪ Ask your correlate manager in R & D: What if your mean-time between new products can be shortened by only one percent? How much value can that add to your operation?

▪ Ask your correlate manager in manufacturing: What if your time-to-market from order entry to shipment can be speeded up by only one percent? How much value can it add to your operation?

▪ Ask your correlate manager in sales or marketing: What if you can identify only one percent more customers for cross-selling only one percent faster or only one percent more accurately? How much value can that add to your operation?

Think of other value-adding opportunities at the "power of one." Help reduce the interest paid on borrowed funds, handle small-production runs more cost-effectively, analyze direct product profitability more accurately or faster, or optimize the mix of leased and owned equipment.

With each opportunity, you need to find out the same three things to determine if you have a fundable value proposition at the "power of one": how much value is deliverable by each proposal, how soon can it start to flow into cash, and how risky is it to go ahead?

## Taking Ownership of Your Values

Performance-based budgeting puts the monkey on your back to take ownership of the values you want to be consistently good at contributing. If you are good at just-in-time inventory management (JIT), you are the owner of valuable operating skills. Their value to management lies in outcomes like these:

- Inventory storage and handling costs can be reduced.
- Insurance, security, and warehousing costs can be reduced.
- Direct costs of borrowing to offset tied-up funds can be reduced.
- Opportunity costs of cash otherwise tied up in inventory can be reduced.

In addition, revenues can be increased from increased sales. An improvement in on-time delivery from 96 to 97 percent for a consumer packaged-goods manufacturer can add $50 million to $80 million in revenues to its retail customers. In turn, the retailers add to the manufacturer's profits by buying more.

If you are good at computer-aided product design (CAD), you are the owner of valuable operating skills. Their value to management lies in outcomes like these:

- New product design and development costs can be reduced.
- Development cycle time can be reduced as developers are

released earlier from each job and reassigned sooner to their next project.

- Time-to-market can be reduced.

In addition, revenues can be increased by filling distribution channels faster so sales cycles can start earlier.

Performance-based budgeting means that you must predict the value of your outcomes before you can get your hands on the budget to perform them. Not only must you predict your final outcomes, but you must also be able to prove to management along the way that their investment is working—that it is "on plan" in making more money for them than they put in. For this reason you must be able to predict milestone-by-milestone outcomes on a periodic basis over the useful life of each project. When top managers ask you if you are on plan or on budget, they want to know if your project's incremental cash flows are accruing with the muchness and soonness that you have predicted. As long as you can say yes, they will leave you alone.

The frequency of your milestone measurements depends on how long a project is going to take to pay back management's investment. A project with a three-month payback should be milestoned with weekly frequency. Monthly value assessments may be adequate for a twelve-month payback. All projects should be front-end loaded with frequent assessments to make sure they get off on plan. In accordance with the rule of no surprises, they should also be milestoned frequently near the end to ensure that all the proposed values are going to be delivered.

Progressive milestone assessments can teach you how much value each type of project can contribute. This will give validity to subsequent predictions for similar projects. You can also learn how soon your values can accrue—how soon a reduction in labor intensity shows up in lower costs and how soon market share grows from improved inventory management or from a faster time-to-market.

Each project's final outcome is your jumping-off value for the next project to continuously improve an operation. How much more value can you add each time? Where can you add it? With what return on investment?

There are three sources of the values you can keep adding.

One is *restorative investments* that correct problems in your operation or someone else's, or get rid of unnecessary costs that have crept in over time. A second is *preventive investments* that allow you to get out in front of a potential problem in sufficient time to head off a competitive disadvantage. The third is *opportunistic investments* that capitalize on your creativity in targeting leads to reduce costs or increase revenues that you find before they find you.

Top management is open to buy all three types of values, twenty-four hours a day. All you have to tell them is how every dollar they invest will perform under your management.

# *Part II*

# Getting the Funds

## Changing the Way You Propose

# 3

# Adhering to Basic Moneymaking Principles and Applying Proven Decision Guidelines

Every top manager will tell you that no two businesses are alike. No matter what you may have learned or done somewhere else, his or her business is different. Yet all top managers adhere to the same two basic principles of evaluating profit-improvement projects, and they apply the same decision guidelines to select the projects they choose to fund.

- All top managers look to see how a project will help circulate capital faster by turning over the assets of their business one or more extra cycles.
- All top managers look to see how much each project contributes to contribution margin and how much it returns on its total investment.

The basic management principle of turning over circulating capital, and the decision guidelines of contribution margin and ROI that tell how much profit the turned-over capital contributes, are articles of faith in how to run a business. Getting your ticket to partnership bucked upstairs depends on how much cash you can help turn over every time you go for funds.

## Adhering to Basic Moneymaking Principles

Two basic principles govern top management decisions about funding. One is to keep money moving. Money in motion makes more money; money at rest incurs opportunity costs. This is the principle of capital circulation. The second principle is that money makes the most money when it turns over fast. This is the principle of turnover.

### The Circulating Capital Principle

Top management's objective in allocating funds is to grow more cash by circulating the cash already on hand through three turns. Each turn adds value, in that:

1. Cash circulates first into inventories.
2. Inventories circulate into receivables.
3. Receivables circulate back into cash, completing one cycle of capital circulation.

Circulating capital is the current assets of a business. They go to work to improve profits as soon as cash is invested to accumulate inventories. Every time raw materials are purchased or processed, inventories come into existence. Another name for production scheduling could be inventory creation. Manufacturing adds to the value of inventories, and so do all the other operating functions of a business that transfer value from cash into products.

Figure 3-1 shows how profits are improved as capital funds circulate. At (A), the funds are in the form of cash. As a project gets under way, the initial cash is transferred into inventories as raw materials are purchased, labor is paid, and finished goods are manufactured and transported from plant to warehouse.

Funds flow from inventories into receivables when sales occur at (B). As they flow, the magnitude of the funds increases because inventories are valued at cost and receivables are valued at their selling price. This increase represents the gross profit on sales. The greater the gross profit rate, the greater the increase in funds during each rotation of the capital circulation cycle.

At (C), the funds earned by the collection of receivables flow

**Figure 3-1.** The circulating capital cycle.

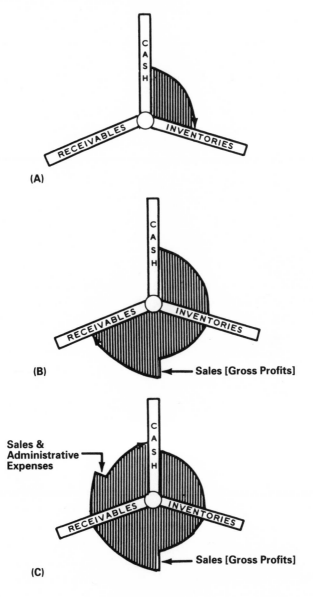

back once again into cash. Before they do, they are reduced by the sales and administrative (S & A) expenses that have been disbursed throughout the cycle.

At this point, one full cycle of capital circulation has been completed. It has resulted in an increase in the number of dollars in the circulating capital fund. This increase is the difference between gross profits and selling and administrative expenses. The more turns of capital during an operating year, the greater the profit.

### The Turnover Principle

The circulation of capital funds takes on meaning only when it relates to time. Faster is more profitable.

Unless your profit projects are focused on improving the turnover of capital employed in your business as quickly as possible—especially capital in the form of inventories—you cannot be a frequent fundee.

Turnover offers virtually unlimited opportunities for profit improvement. The most common way to improve turnover is through increased sales volume and lowered operating-fund requirements, which is the same as saying lowered circulating capital. In some situations, turnover may be improved by decreasing sales or even by increasing the investment in operating assets.

As Figure 3-2 shows, the drive wheel that makes capital move is sales. This is why revenue generation must always be your focal point—either increasing sales or reducing the cost of sales.

At the point where the optimal relationship exists between sales volume and the investment in operating funds required to achieve it, the turnover rate yields the best profit.

In Figure 3-2, the circumference of the sales wheel represents $200,000 worth of sales during a twelve-month operating period. The sales wheel drives the smaller wheel of circulating capital. The circumference of the circulating capital wheel equals $100,000 invested in working funds. Enclosing the circulating capital wheel is a larger wheel, also driven by sales, that represents circulating capital of $100,000 plus another $100,000 invested in plant and facilities, equaling total capital employed. The circumference of the wheel representing total capital employed is, therefore, $200,000—equal to the sales drive wheel.

**Figure 3-2.** The turnover cycle.

### Basic Relationship

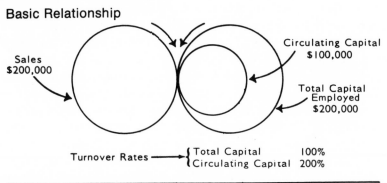

### Option A: Increase Sales

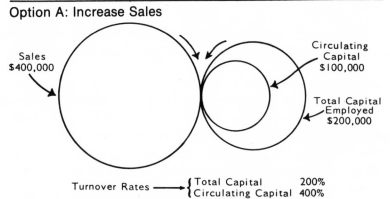

### Option B: Decrease Capital

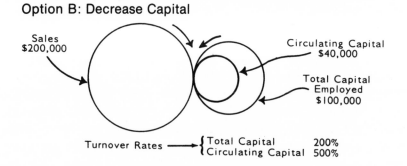

When annual sales are $200,000 and total capital employed is $200,000, the annual turnover rate of total funds invested is 100 percent, or one turn per year. The circulating capital portion of the total, amounting to $100,000, will turn over at the rate of 200 percent, or twice a year.

Each of the three components of circulating capital—cash, receivables, and inventories—has its own individual turnover rate. Inventory turnover is calculated according to the number of months' supply on hand. A six-month supply represents two turns per year, or a 200 percent annual turnover rate. Turnover of receivables is expressed as the number of days of business outstanding. If ninety days of business are outstanding, the receivables turnover is four turns per year, or 400 percent. Increasing turnover reduces the amount of funds invested in working assets, which reduces the total asset base.

You have two strategies to improve turnover. Option A increases sales. Option B decreases the amount of money invested in circulating capital. Figure 3-2 shows an opportunity to double sales to $400,000 per year without increasing the $200,000 of total funds employed in the business. This is option A. The turnover rate will increase from 100 to 200 percent. At the same time, the turnover rate of circulating capital will increase from 200 to 400 percent.

If you cannot increase sales, option B offers an alternative opportunity to improve turnover. Even though sales remain at the same annual rate of $200,000, turnover can be increased if total capital employed in working assets is reduced from $200,000 to $100,000. This includes a parallel reduction in circulating capital from $100,000 to $40,000. These reductions help improve two turnover rates: Total capital employed goes from 100 to 200 percent and circulating capital goes from 200 to 500 percent.

The profit improvement created by options A and B can be calculated by multiplying the increase in funds generated at each turn of the operating cycle by the number of turns. If the operating profit from one turn in the basic relationship shown in Figure 3-2 is $50,000, the profit realized by option A doubles to $100,000. In option B, profit remains at $50,000 but $100,000 of funds are released from operations that can be used to generate additional business or reduce debt.

Total funds employed at any given time is the sum of circulating and fixed capital funds. An improvement in their turnover will correspondingly improve the turnover of total funds employed. You can target any component of the turnover mix without having to consider any of the others or their sum total. Exclusive of reducing receivables or working assets, improvement in the turnover of any single item in inventory will improve total turnover and consequently contribute to profit improvement.

Accounts receivable and inventory are the two major current assets of every business. By being turned over, current assets are more quickly convertible to cash than fixed assets. Anything you can do to speed up asset turnover in receivables or inventory will make money. If you allow these assets to build up—if sales decline and inventories grow or if customers delay paying their bills—you will be helping to lose money, not make it.

Every day that you can condense the receivables collection period puts money in the bank. Every additional turn of inventory also improves profits. An item that turns over 1.7 times a year sits in inventory approximately seven months before being sold. If you can help move it out in six months instead of seven, using the "power of one," you can accelerate its contribution to earnings by one-seventh.

## Applying Decision Guidelines to Improve Profits

Each time you put forward a proposal to fund a profit-improvement project, your top managers categorize it according to four values—its dollar value, its time value, its risk value, and its opportunity value—as follows:

1. How much cash flow the project proposes to generate when its costs are subtracted from its benefits.
2. How long it will take to make cash flow turn positive, which is the time it takes for the project's investment to achieve payback. After payback, profits can increase at a faster rate than sales since fixed costs are fully recovered.
3. How much risk is involved, which is directly proportional to how much cash flow the project proposes and how long it takes to turn positive. If the risk of failing to receive the

proposed cash flow is significant, what is the most likely cost of failure and what is the earliest point in time at which the investment can be stopped, the loss can be cut, and the project dropped?

4. How much opportunity cost may be incurred by not making the investment or delaying it.

A project that earns enough brownie points to be categorized as "take a second look" gets the next three guidelines applied to it to see if it maximizes cash flow, minimizes the time it takes to turn cash flow positive, and minimizes risk and opportunity cost:

1. Management analyzes the project's contribution margin.
2. They apply the return-on-investment principle to the project's cash flow.
3. They calculate the project's net present value.

### Contribution Margin Guidelines

Contribution margin is a variation on cash flow analysis. Cash flow analysis sums up all the cash revenues from sales generated by a project and subtracts its operating expenses. Contribution margin calculates the margin contributed by sales. It takes the cash flow from sales and subtracts the variable costs required to earn them.

Unlike cash flow analysis to show revenue contribution, contribution margin tells you how much margin is contributed by each dollar of revenues. The margin first goes to cover the project's fixed operating overhead until the investment breaks even. After that, margin becomes profit.

If a project's total contribution margin is $.095, this means that each $1 of sales contributes a margin of 9.5 cents to cover fixed operating overhead. When enough dollars of sales contribute enough 9.5 cents of margin, the project breaks even. In order to increase the contribution from sales, volume must be stepped up at the current margin or the project's variable costs must be reduced at the current sales volume.

In projects with a high contribution margin—40 percent or more—only a small improvement in volume is required for large profits. Low-margin projects below 15 percent require large changes in volume to improve profits.

Figures 3-3 through 3-5 show three ways to look at contribution margin. Figure 3-3 shows contribution margin in operating statement terms. Figure 3-4 shows it according to its sources in the lines of business that generate it. Figure 3-5 shows it in relation to sales.

Figure 3-6 applies contribution margin to three product lines. Line A's high contribution margin suggests profit-improvement projects that increase sales volume. Line B requires reductions of its variable costs.

### Return-on-Investment (ROI) Guidelines

By comparing the average income gained or expenses saved to the cash outlay made to fund a project, the percentage rate of return from making the investment can be calculated.

Two strategies drive ROI. One is to increase sales in order to drive the circulation of capital. Capital increases every time it circulates. If you cannot find a project to increase sales, try the second ROI strategy. Look for a project to reduce or avoid costs. Cost reduction can come from reduced costs of sales, reduced selling and administrative expenses, or a reduced sales cycle. Cost displacement can come from buying or outsourcing instead of making or from leasing instead of buying, both of which seek to trade off a larger cost for a smaller one.

Return on investment can be calculated in four ways:

1. As the income generated per dollar invested, which results in a dollar figure called *return on investment* (ROI).
2. As an average annual percentage return per dollar invested over the life of a project, which results in a percentage called *internal rate of return* (IRR).
3. As an average after-tax profit over the life of a project divided by the investment, which results in a percentage called *accounting rate of return* (AROR).
4. As a project's profit before taxes, divided by the capital employed in inventories, accounts receivable, and net invest-

*(text continues on page 62)*

**Figure 3-3.** Contribution margin in operating statement terms.

| | | |
|---|---|---|
| Sales (50,000 units @ $80) | $4,000,000 | 100.0% |
| Cost of goods manufactured and sold: | | |
| Variable manufacturing costs (50,000 units @ $10) | 500,000 | 12.5 |
| Manufacturing contribution margin | 3,500,000 | 87.5% |
| Selling and administrative expenses: | | |
| Variable selling and administrative expenses (50,000 units @ $5) | 250,000 | 6.25 |
| Contribution margin | $3,250,000 | 81.25% |

**Figure 3-4.** Contribution margin by line of business.

| | Total | A | B | C | D |
|---|---|---|---|---|---|
| Number of units sold | 396,000 | 32,000 | 100,000 | 84,000 | 180,000 |
| Selling price per unit | $ 14.80AV | $15.00 | $8.00 | $16.00 | $18.00 |
| Variable manufacturing cost* | 6.06AV | 9.80 | 4.90 | 9.60 | 4.40 |
| Variable selling and administrative expense | .57AV | 1.00 | .18 | 1.00 | .50 |
| Contribution margin | $ 8.17AV | $ 4.20 | $2.92 | $ 5.40 | $13.10 |
| Total fixed costs | $ 1,726,000 | | | | |

NOTE: AV = average of product lines.
*Materials, factory supplies, labor, other variable costs.

**Figure 3-5.** Contribution margin in relation to sales.

| Product Line | % Total Sales | % Product Line Contribution Margin on Sales | % Product Line Contribution Margin to Total |
|---|---|---|---|
| A | 8.2 | 27.9 | 4.1 |
| B | 13.6 | 36.5 | 9.0 |
| C | 22.9 | 33.8 | 14.0 |
| D | 55.3 | 72.8 | 72.9 |
| Total | 100.0 | 52.2* | 100.0 |

*Average contribution margin on total sales.

**Figure 3-6.** Contribution margin by product line.

| | Total | | Product Lines [$000] | | |
| --- | --- | --- | --- | --- | --- |
| | | A | B | C | |
| 1. Sales | $2,600.0 | $1,742.0 | $650.0 | $208.0 | |
| | 100.0% | 67.0% | 25.0% | 8.0% | |
| 2. Cost of sales | $2,106.0 | $1,440.0 | $520.0 | $146.0 | |
| | 81.0% | 82.7% | 80.0% | 70.0% | |
| 3. Gross profit (1 − 2) | $ 494.0 | $ 302.0 | $ 130.0 | $ 62.0 | |
| | 19.0% | 17.3% | 20.0% | 30.0% | |
| 4. Wages | $ 221.0 | $ 134.0 | $ 65.0 | $ 22.0 | |
| | 8.5% | 7.7% | 10.0% | 10.5% | |
| 5. Other | $ 26.0 | $ 10.0 | $ 13.0 | $ 3.0 | |
| | 1.0% | 0.6% | 1.9% | 1.5% | |
| 6. Total (4 + 5) | $ 247.0 | $ 144.0 | $ 78.0 | $ 25.0 | |
| | 9.5% | 8.3% | 11.9% | 12.0% | |
| 7. Contribution margin (3 − 6) | $ 247.0 | $ 158.0 | $ 52.0 | $ 37.0 | |
| | 9.5% | 9.0% | 8.1% | 18.0% | |

ment, which results in a percentage called *return on capital employed* (ROCE).

Top management's sole economic justification for investing in your profit-improvement projects is to earn a superior rate of return on the funds invested. A superior return can be achieved in two ways. One is in income gained; the other is in costs avoided in obtaining investment funds, costs of retaining such funds, and costs incurred by denying funds for alternative, potentially more profitable projects.

As Figure 3-7 shows, ROI is the product of the rate of operating profit expressed as a percentage of sales and the rate of turnover. Any time you want to improve ROI, you must increase either your operating rate or turnover.

Figure 3-7 shows the components of ROI expressed as turnover. If you recommend a project to reduce receivables, this reduces the amount of funds invested in working asssets. By reducing the total investment base, you can improve profit without increasing sales volume.

Figure 3-8 shows options for increasing operating profit. A project to lower the cost of sales reduces total costs and thereby increases operating profit.

The short way to calculate ROI is by combining the two figures into a single formula with a single message: You can improve ROI by reducing total assets or increasing sales.

$$\frac{\text{Net operating profit}}{\text{Sales}} \times \frac{\text{Profit on sales}}{\text{Total funds invested}}$$

[or]

$$\frac{\text{Incremental net profits}}{\text{Incremental net investment}}$$

### Net Present Value (NPV) Guidelines

Net present value (NPV) measures the current value of future cash flows that will accrue beyond the first year of a project's life—a time called "the future." NPV discounts future cash back to

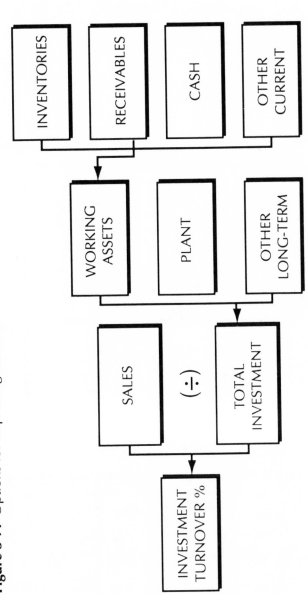

**Figure 3-7.** Options for improving turnover.

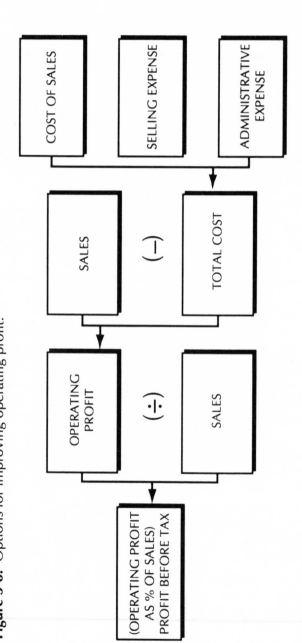

**Figure 3-8.** Options for improving operating profit.

its equivalent worth today. This smooths out the effects of time on money, which makes a dollar tomorrow worth less than the same dollar today.

A positive net present value is a standard acceptance criterion for profit-improvement projects.

NPV brings future cash flows back to their present value by factoring them with a discount rate called the cost of capital, management's minimum rate of return for approving an investment. This is why cost of capital is referred to as the "hurdle rate."

Hurdle rates are management's attempts to reduce risk. They act as guidelines to minimum internal rates of return that can be safely lived with for various types of investments. Low-risk investments such as a simple product-line extension may have a hurdle rate of only 10 percent. At the other extreme, high-risk investments such as new-product introductions into new markets may have to clear a hurdle rate of 20 to 30 percent. Medium-risk investment opportunities fall in between.

Net present value is expressed by the formula:

$$\text{Future cash flow} \times \text{discount factor} = \text{NPV}.$$

Time eats value alive. If today's dollar, which is worth 100 cents, is discounted at 10 percent over the next twenty-four months, 14 cents will be eaten up by time. One hundred cents will become 86 cents—almost a 20 percent loss. A five-year table of present values is shown in Figure A–1 in Appendix A.

By calculating a project's NPV, you can determine whether it is more cost-effective to make an investment in it, put your money elsewhere, or let your money sit idle even though it incurs opportunity cost. According to NPV, investing $50 million for future cash flows valued today at $59.755 million is an acceptable investment because you are paying $50 million for assets worth $59.755 million. This earns you $9.755 million in new value.

Figure 3-9 shows the cash flow forecasts and time-value calculations for a typical proposal to invest in a new project when top management's alternative is to do nothing—that is, to maintain liquidity rather than invest because there is nothing better to invest in. A discount rate of 10 percent is assumed as the cost of capital.

The proposed project will cost $500 in year 0, and cash operat-

**Figure 3-9.** Net present value calculation.

| Year | Benefits | Costs | Cash Flow | PV of $1 @ 10% | Discounted Cash Flow |
|------|----------|-------|-----------|----------------|----------------------|
| 0 | $ 0 | $ (500) | $(500) | 1.000 | $(500) |
| 0–1 | 425 | (200) | 225 | .952 | 214 |
| 1–2 | 425 | (200) | 225 | .861 | 194 |
| 2–3 | 350 | (200) | 150 | .779 | 117 |
| 3–4 | 250 | (200) | 50 | .705 | 35 |
| TOTAL | $1,450 | $(1,300) | $ 150 | | $ 60 NPV |

ing expenses will be $200 per year for four years. The cash benefits start out positive but decline over the four years to total $1,450, leaving a net positive cash flow over the life of the project of $150 before discounting. When the cash-flow forecasts are made equivalent in time by multiplying each annual cash flow by the present value for each period, the net present value comes to $60. The proposed investment is better than doing nothing because all costs are covered, the 10 percent cost of capital is realized, and the project will yield a $60 return.

Depending on the cash flow or the discount rate, the NPV of $60 could be negative or zero. If the NPV were zero, earnings would equal the cost of capital at 10 percent. If there were no competitive projects, and the only alternative were to do nothing, a proposal with an NPV of zero would be acceptable because top management would earn the cost of capital. If NPV were negative because of inadequate cash flow, the proposal would be unacceptable because it would earn less than 10 percent.

## Netting out the Decision Process

If there are any tricks of the trade that top management uses in netting out decisions on what projects to fund and how much to fund them, the following incremental investment standards cover most of them:

- Primary objective is long-term capital appreciation.
- Focus is on total return—the aggregate return from capital appreciation.
- Emphasis is on consistency of growth by avoidance of volatility in annual values.
- Total return must meet or exceed minimum incremental rate of return (IRR). For many businesses, minimum IRR starts at 100 percent.
- In a pinch any incremental investment is OK if it generates more cash flow than the cost of the capital that goes into it.
- Minimize the capital invested in each project.
- Keep capital continuously employed.

Using these standards, a "good deal" is easy to spot when it comes along:

- It improves contribution margin.
- It improves inventory or receivables turnover.
- It improves circulation of capital.
- It reduces, eliminates, or displaces costs.

Taken at face value, criteria like these suggest that top managers could invest in any of your proposals that keep capital turning over at a positive net present value. But in the real world, managers are constrained by practical limits on the capital expenditures they feel they can make. They look for proposals that can maximize net present value and still stay within their self-imposed capital limitations. Some managers use a profitability index. They compare the net present value of each project with its investment:

$$\frac{\text{Net present value}}{\text{Investment}} = \text{Profitability index}$$

When a profitability index is used to make go/no-go decisions on funding, proposals with the highest promise of profit contribution are selected first, as in this example:

Management is presented with two projects—one from you—to increase sales revenues, both of which propose to raise profits on sales by an identical 10 percent with an investment of $100,000. Management selects project A because it improves sales contribution by $100,000 more than project B. The calculations look like this:

*Project A:*

$100,000 investment = $30,000 profit on $300,000 of incremental sales

This represents a 30 percent return on each dollar invested, with capital appreciation of 300 percent.

*Project B:*

$100,000 investment = $20,000 profit on $200,000 of incremental sales

This represents a 20 percent return on each dollar invested, with capital appreciation of 200 percent.

But in reality, the project As of the world do not always get the funds. Top managers assess their risk within a range of subjective probabilities for failure. If project A has a higher degree of risk, project B may get the funds.

Proposals have different degrees of risk and managers have different levels of uncertainty. Some proposals are relative no-brainers. They can be evaluated with a good deal of accuracy. Their projected benefits are practically assured. Many managers simply put their OK on zero-risk proposals like these whenever the net present value exceeds the cost of capital.

At other times or with other managers, no-brainers that are not on management's "must list" and propose a 10 percent return will be passed over for a higher risk proposal promising a 50 percent return because management feels it "must" be in a new field or wants to shed a stolid image. Another constraint on approving no-brainers is management's concern about whether the business can handle a proposal's requirements with current capabilities or fear that a project may make excessive demands on top-level oversight.

Managers at the top are consummate jugglers of risk and reward, seesawing between "what if we do?" and "what if we don't?" Some managers think of reward first and risk second. Managers with such a go-go mind-set are likely to be entrepreneurs whose attitude can be summed up as "I like risk. That's where you make money." But for most corporate managers, risk control is the name of the game.

Top managers see themselves as stewards of stockholder faith. This prejudices them to divide risk into small, survivable bites and manage with a conservative style that favors certainty over chance, incremental gains over breakthroughs, and consistency over flashes in the pan. Life at the top is a world where faster payback is often more acceptable than bigger payout; where a smaller but surer payout can be more acceptable than a bigger payout; where opportunity costs that may be incurred at some time in the future are generally more acceptable than smaller direct costs incurred today.

Top management's fixation on conserving the critical mass of the business is reflected in points of view like these:

- How would I feel about investing $100 million with a fifty-fifty chance of losing it or making $500 million? Most likely, I'd end up making less than the maximum, maybe $200 or $300 million. But if it were a case of $500 million or broke, I would seldom elect to take it even at fifty-fifty.

- When I have a high-risk decision, I make it divisible. If the total risk were $150 million, with a 10 percent chance of losing it and a 90 percent chance of making $500 million, I would risk $15 million to the point of first withdrawal—if it is our kind of technology and we know what to do with it so we can take a higher risk. If it is not our own technology, I would risk $5 million on step one with a 15 percent or so expectation of success. After spending a second $5 million, we might have a 90 percent expectation. Now we can put in $25 million. If a competitor gets in first while we're pussyfooting around, we might have only a $100 million business instead of $500 million. But we would still get some of it. The important thing is that we are not betting the business.

- In the end, how much of a gamble I would take depends on how much money is involved—$25 million is one thing, but $250 million is something else. I would risk the smaller number but not the larger one. If I lose $250 million, it would mar earnings.

# 4

# Making a Business
# Case for Funds

A business case proposes the return for being funded. It is your promissory note to management.

A promise has the best chance of being funded when it meets three requirements:

1. *Optimizes management's value* in its added cash flow.
2. *Minimizes management's time-to-payback* in returning its investment.
3. *Maximizes management's sureness* in receiving the projected cash flow in the amount and at the time it has been promised.

There are two kinds of business cases: revenue improvement and cost reduction. Revenue-improvement projects make their business case on two comparisons:

1. Future revenues will be improved over current revenues.
2. Future revenues will return more than the investment required to produce them.

Cost-reduction projects make their business case on two similar comparisons:

1. Future costs will be reduced over current costs.
2. Future cost savings will return more than the investment required to produce them.

Future revenue gains and future cost savings represent your values. When you make a business case for funding, it must be because your current contributions of value cannot be improved without incremental investment. If you have to defend against a reduction in funds, it must be because your current contributions of value cannot be sustained with a reduced investment.

## Proposing Profit Improvement

A business case for funds is known as a Profit Improvement Proposal (PIP), a proposal to improve the profit contributed by a business operation to a business. Because it proposes to add value, a PIP is also called a value proposition. By whatever name, a PIP is *an offer to sell a claim on a future cash flow*. The claim is yours. The investment that purchases the claim and holds the owner's stake in it comes from your top management.

If a business case were to be summarized as a narrative proposition, it would have you say something like this to top management:

> You have such and such business objective. We can help you realize it better or faster or more surely. The way our operation stands now, your objective is being constrained by unnecessary costs that we have or by our inability to help you bring in additional available revenues. What if we can help advance your objective by this many dollars in this much time by reducing some of these costs or helping to realize some of these revenues?

If you are an internal service function, your proposition can help improve your own contribution or the contribution that some other operation now makes to a top management objective. For example, as an IT manager for a retailer, you can say:

> What if we can help you reach your objective three months sooner to be able to finance 500 new stores this year? We propose to do this by enabling each existing store to contribute an additional $200,000. Approxi-

mately $100,000 of this money will come from average cost savings per store as a result of computer-assisted checkout stations. The other $100,000 will come from eliminating the cost of correcting current checker errors. For every store that is on a growth track, total annual savings equal an average week's gross sales—the equivalent of giving you the revenues of a fifty-three–week operating year by reducing the cost to operate during the normal fifty-two weeks.

When it comes to going for funds, the entry fee just to get in the door is that whatever proposal you hold in your hand must be what is called "cash-neutral" or better. *Cash-neutral* means that management breaks even if it goes for your deal. No cost is incurred. What goes out comes back, ideally with enough interest earned to pay for any opportunity cost and the time value of the money while the investment was at risk.

Cash-neutral is not really a standard; it is the floor from which monetary standards of performance begin. No business puts money out just to get it back. Managers are money makers, not currency exchangers who are content to trade off one dollar for another one. But as a floor, cash-neutral tells you how management really looks at its money: No cost is a good cost; all costs are to be avoided; the best costs are zero costs.

In every top manager's mind, a penny saved is much more than a penny earned. It is the residue of many more pennies that must be earned in order to end up with a penny after the costs to make it *and* the taxes that are taken away from what it makes are accounted for.

Making a business case for funding is a six-part process:

1. Link up with a strategic business objective.
2. Diagnose a competitively disadvantaging problem or an unrealized opportunity for competitive advantage.
3. Prescribe a more competitively advantaged outcome.
4. Cost the benefits of the improved cash flows and diagram the improved work flows that contribute to them.
5. Team the project.
6. Maintain partnered accountability upstairs.

### Part 1: Link up With a Strategic Business Objective

Target a strategic business to which top management has committed funds. A strategic business is a profit-centered line of business (LOB), whose revenues and earnings are critical to management's success. Fit your proposal into management's commitment by positioning yourself as an enabler that can help achieve it more cost-effectively, faster, or with greater certainty. Summarize your proposed contributions to the strategic objective's competitive advantage by quantifying how much you can contribute and how soon.

If you manage an internal service function, you can also link up with a strategic business objective by proposing an improved contribution to another manager's operation that represents a core capability for achieving the strategic objective.

### Part 2: Diagnose a Competitively Disadvantaging Problem or an Unrealized Opportunity for Competitive Advantage

Survey the work flows and their resulting cash flows of the strategic business. Diagnose where it is competitively disadvantaged and by how much. Illustrate the contributing work-flow problem that you can help improve on a process flow chart. Summarize its impacts on cash flow: the unnecessary costs it adds or the unrealized revenues it causes.

### Part 3: Prescribe a More Competitively Advantaged Outcome

Bring forward four highlights from the cost-benefit analysis in part 4 that summarize your prescription for improved profits:

1. Net present value of your proposed incremental profit contribution
2. Incremental investment required to fund the incremental profits
3. Internal rate of return on the investment
4. Time to payback of the investment

## Part 4: Cost the Benefits of the Improved Cash Flows and Diagram the Improved Work Flows That Contribute to Them

Calculate the costs and benefits of your proposed improvement. If your improvement can be fully realized within one year, use the model Single-Year Cost-Benefit Analysis shown in Figure 4-1. An expanded version is shown in Figure 4-2. If your improvement requires more than one year to be fully realized, use the Multiyear Cost-Benefit Analysis shown in Figure 4-3. Guidelines for its completion are specified in Figure 4-4.

Back up the cost-benefit analysis with a process flow chart of the improved work flows that contribute to the improved cash flows. Figure 4-5 shows a typical process flow chart. The improved work flows "prove" the cash benefits by showing where they come from. For example, what work flows have you eliminated, condensed, or combined? What systems of work flows have you reintegrated into new networking? What processes have you reengineered for faster cycle times? What work have you removed from a process by outsourcing?

What assets are you leasing instead of purchasing to help conserve the funds required for the project?

With a lease, you give up the rights that go with ownership, but you also give up most of the risks of ownership: sunk costs that create a debt, along with maintenance costs and obsolescence.

The comparative cash flows under leasing and buying usually determine the choice between them. In an outright purchase, the cash outflows consist of the initial purchase price or, if the purchase funds are borrowed, the principal and interest on the loan. Cash inflows are the amount of the loan, tax benefits from yearly interest and depreciation, and salvage value. A lease's cash outflows are its yearly rental fee, which is fully tax-deductible. There are no cash inflows with a lease, since there are none of the residual or salvage values that come with ownership.

Comparing the cash flows is a two-step process. First, calculate the annual cash flows from outright purchase and from leasing, as Figure 4-6 shows. Then compare them by calculating their discounted cash flow (DCF)—in other words, their present value—to determine which option yields the greater cash benefit.

All the definitions and calculations on the model cost-benefit

**Figure 4-1.** Single-year cost-benefit analysis.

INCREMENTAL INVESTMENT

1. Cost of proposed equipment/system     $ _____
2. PLUS: installation costs     _____
3. PLUS: investment in other assets required     _____
4. MINUS: avoidable costs (repairs & remodeling)     _____
5. MINUS: Net after-tax adjustment for sale of properties retired as result of investment     _____
6. TOTAL INVESTMENT (sum of 1–5)     _____

COSTS-BENEFITS

|  | *Proposal* | *Present or Competitive* | *± Difference* |
|---|---|---|---|
| 7. Sales revenue | $_____ | $_____ | $_____ |
| MINUS: variable costs: | | | |
| 8. Labor (including fringe benefits) | _____ | _____ | _____ |
| 9. Materials | _____ | _____ | _____ |
| 10. Maintenance | _____ | _____ | _____ |
| 11. Other variable costs | _____ | _____ | _____ |
| 12. TOTAL VARIABLE COSTS | _____ | _____ | _____ |
| 13. Contribution margin (sum of 7 + 12) | _____ | _____ | _____ |
| MINUS: fixed costs: | | | |
| 14. Rent or depreciation on equipment | _____ | _____ | _____ |
| 15. Other fixed costs | _____ | _____ | _____ |
| 16. TOTAL FIXED COSTS | _____ | _____ | _____ |
| 17. Net income before taxes | _____ | _____ | _____ |

**Figure 4-1.** (continued)

---

ACCOUNTING RATE OF RETURN ON PROPOSED INVESTMENT

18. Total investment cost       $_____
    (line 6 or total
    capitalized annual cost of
    system)
19. Net income before taxes for     $_____
    year (17)
20. Before-tax rate of return (line      _____%
    19 + 20)

---

analysis apply equally to cash purchases and leases. The calculation of net present value is the same. There are three major differences:

1. There is no total investment under lease. Cash flow benefits begin immediately on day 1 of year 0.
2. Payback does not apply under lease unless there is an option to purchase.
3. IRR is replaced by the lease rate charged.

Cash flow is generally the main determinant in deciding whether to lease or buy. Several other facts may affect its importance:

- A lease offers 100 percent financing.
- Lease obligations are not reflected on the corporate balance sheet.
- Rents are tax-deductible.
- In the early years of a lease, rental payments are generally lower than the combined interest expense and depreciation of ownership.
- A lease may be renewed at termination or its interest rate may be renegotiated if rates decrease.
- Obsolete equipment may be enhanced or exchanged under lease.

A major benefit of leasing is that it helps reduce the assets you must have under management. The fewer assets you have to

*(text continues on page 80)*

**Figure 4-2.** Single-year cost-benefit analysis (expanded from Figure 4-1).

| STAGE 1. INCREMENTAL INVESTMENT ANALYSIS | | |
|---|---|---|
| 1. Cost of proposed equipment | $ 39,600 | |
| Estimated installation cost | 6,000 | |
| Subtotal | 45,600 | |
| Minus initial tax benefit of | 3,190 | |
| Total | | 42,410 |
| 2. Disposal value of equipment to be replaced | 8,000 | |
| Capital additions required in absence of proposed equipment | 6,000 | |
| Minus initial tax benefit for capital additions of | 420 | |
| Total | | $13,580 |
| 3. Incremental investment (1 − 2) | | $28,830 |

| STAGE 2. PROFIT-IMPROVEMENT ANALYSIS (ANNUAL CONTRIBUTION) | |
|---|---|
| 4. Profit improvement—net decrease in operating costs (from line 27) | $24,952 |
| 5. Profit improvement—net increase in revenue (from line 31) | |
| 6. Annual profit improvement (lines 4 + 5) | $24,952 |

**STAGE 3. NEXT-YEAR OPERATING BENEFITS FROM PROPOSED EQUIPMENT**

**A. Effect of Proposed Equipment on Operating Costs**

| *(Computed on Machine-Hour Basis)* | *Present* | *Proposed* |
|---|---|---|
| 7. Direct labor (wages plus incentives and bonuses) | $ 10.50 | $ 3.50 |
| 8. Indirect labor (supervision, inspectors, helpers) | 3.67 | 1.22 |
| 9. Fringe benefits (vacations, pensions, insurance) | 2.15 | 0.72 |

| | | |
|---|---|---|
| 10. Maintenance (ordinary only, parts and labor) | 1.18 | 0.90 |
| 11. Abrasives, media, compounds, or other consumable supplies | 1.32 | 1.10 |
| 12. Power | 0.56 | 0.48 |
| 13. Total (sum of 7 through 12) | $ 19.38 | $ 7.92 |
| 14. Estimated machine hours to be operated next year | 2,400 | 3,000 |
| 15. Partial operating costs next year (13 × 14) | $46,512 (A) | $23,760 (B) |
| 16. Partial operating profit improvement (15A − 15B) | | $22,752 |

| (Computed on a Yearly Basis) | Increase | Decrease |
|---|---|---|
| 17. Scrap or damaged work | $ | $ 700 |
| 18. Downtime | | 1,500 |
| 19. Floor space | | |
| 20. Subcontracting | | |
| 21. Inventory | | |
| 22. Safety | | |
| 23. Flexibility | | |
| 24. Other | | |
| 25. Total | $ (A) | $ 2,200 (B) |
| 26. Net decrease in operating costs (partial) (25B − 25A) | | $ 2,200 |
| 27. Total effect of proposed equipment on operating costs (16 + 26) | | $24,952 |

## B. Effect of Proposed Equipment on Revenue

| (Computed on Yearly Basis) | Increase | Decrease |
|---|---|---|
| 28. From change in quality of products | $ | $ |
| 29. From change in volume of output | | |
| 30. Total | $ (A) | $ (B) |
| 31. Net increase in revenue (30A − 30B) | | $ |

*(continues)*

**Figure 4-2.** (continued)

| STAGE 4. ANALYSIS OF RETURN ON INCREMENTAL INVESTMENT | |
|---|---:|
| 32. Incremental investment (line 3) | $28,830 |
| 33. Annual profit improvement (line 6) | $24,952 |
| 34. Before-tax return on investment (line 33 ÷ line 32) | 86% |

manage, yet the more cash flow you can generate with them, the better an asset manager you will be.

### Part 5: Team the Project

Use Figure 4-7 as a model to assign the principal players to your project team, along with vendor or systems integrator players you ally with as business partners.

### Part 6: Maintain Partnered Accountability Upstairs

Pledge your business partnership with top management by committing to continuous periodic measurement of real-time results on a milestone-by-milestone timetable. Report by exception to avoid surprises. Upstairs, no news is good news. Preview your next one or two profit-improvement projects—the one you are preheating in the oven and another that you are storing in the freezer—in order to ensure continuous improvement and alert management to the future funds you will be claiming.

Partnership at the top is a no-excuses, no-surprises alliance. You must support your top-management partners' objectives and provide an increment to their achievement. You must deliver your incremental contributions on time every time, which requires you to make "reliability" your new middle name.

## Proposing With Minimal Data

Profit-improvement opportunities are more likely to be lost by waiting "to get everything right" than for any other reason. No

**Figure 4-3.** Multiyear cost-benefit analysis.

| INVESTMENT | Y 0 | Y 1 | Y 2 | Y 3 | Y 4 | Y 5 |
|---|---|---|---|---|---|---|
| 1. New equipment<br>2. Annual maintenance<br>3. Implementation<br>4. Site preparation | | | | | | |
| 5. TOTAL INVESTMENT<br>(CASH OUT) | | | | | | |

| CONTRIBUTION FROM SALES | Y 1 | Y 2 | Y 3 | Y 4 | Y 5 |
|---|---|---|---|---|---|
| 6. Increased revenues<br>7. Less increased costs of sales | | | | | |
| 8 NET CASH IN (6 − 7) | | | | | |

| CONTRIBUTION FROM REDUCED COSTS | Y 1 | Y 2 | Y 3 | Y 4 | Y 5 |
|---|---|---|---|---|---|
| 9. Fixed costs<br>10. Variable costs | | | | | |
| 11. NET CASH IN (9 + 10) | | | | | |

| NET CASH FLOWS | Y 0 | Y 1 | Y 2 | Y 3 | Y 4 | Y 5 |
|---|---|---|---|---|---|---|
| 12. Cumulative cash flow | | | | | | |
| 13. TOTAL PROFIT IMPROVEMENT [(8 + 11) − 5] | | | | | | |

| | |
|---|---|
| NET PRESENT VALUE (NPV) ($) | _____ |
| DISCOUNT RATE (%) | ____ |
| PAYBACK ☐ YR 1 ☐ YR 2 ☐ YR 3 | |
| INTERNAL RATE OF RETURN (IRR) % | ____ |

**Figure 4-4.** Cost-benefit analysis guidelines.

| | |
|---|---|
| Item 5: | TOTAL INVESTMENT represents total incremental expenditures to obtain the benefits, including capital equipment and materials, software, services other than annual maintenance, training, and other variable costs that are expensed. Total investment is assumed to be a one-time cost that will be paid out in full in Year 0. (Total investment is the "cost" in the cost-benefit analysis.) |

Multiply the total investment in capital equipment by the current depreciation rate permitted by the Accelerated Cost Recovery Schedule (ACRS). Subtract the resulting cash flows generated by cumulative annual depreciation from the total investment.

Item 2: ANNUAL MAINTENANCE represents a recurrent fixed annual cost that will be incurred throughout the useful life of the total investment.

Item 13: TOTAL PROFIT IMPROVEMENT represents the added-value benefits from: (1) savings from avoidance, reduction, or elimination of variable costs, and (2) revenues from expanded sales.

On a worksheet, itemize each source and its contribution to savings that results in a positive cash flow: reductions in fully burdened labor and materials, energy, and reduction of inventory carrying costs and interest on the capital invested in inventory (although not on reduction of inventory alone).

Also itemize each source and its contribution to revenues that results in a positive cash flow: expanded gross margins from increased sales or increased unit margins that are calculated after subtracting manufacturing and marketing costs. Overhead costs associated with increased sales will probably not expand proportionately, if at all.

Item 12: CUMULATIVE CASH FLOW represents the incremental cash benefits generated by savings and revenues. They are calculated on a recurrent annual basis that can be accumulated at the end of the useful life of the total investment. (Cash flow is the "benefits" in the cost-benefit analysis.)

Item 16: PAYBACK is the year in which the cumulative cash flows return the total investment, releasing the investor from risk. After payback, cash flows become positive and profits occur. Payback is calculated by dividing total investment by cumulative cash flow.

Item 14: NET PRESENT VALUE (NPV) represents current value of the sum of all future cash flows after they have been discounted for annual opportunity cost based on what the same total investment might have saved or earned if invested elsewhere. Annual opportunity

---

cost is calculated over the useful life of the total investment. For example, the Year 1 net present value of $50,000 by the time it will be received in Year 2 is $41,667, which represents $50,000 discounted by the factor of 0.83333.

Item 17: INTERNAL RATE OF RETURN (IRR) represents the ratio of total profit improvement to the total investment required to generate it. IRR must equal or exceed the minimum hurdle rate for incremental investments, generally set at 2/3 to 3/3 of the cost of capital.

---

matter how long you take to get ready, you will never get everything right. But the longer you take, the greater risk you run of having your opportunity window close on your fingers while they are still counting the latest iteration of data. This does no good for your reputation for reliability.

Two things are worth remembering:

1. There is no such thing as an exact number. All numbers are approximations. Get as close as you can as fast as you can and go with the numbers you have.
2. Top management wants "good enough" numbers. All they must do is represent what is most likely to happen in the future if management makes an investment decision in your favor today.

In order to produce a continuing impact on management's profitability, you need to learn to live with minimal data and to know what minimal means. Data are minimally sufficient when you know enough about the current values of a problem or opportunity to know that you can make a cost-effective improvement in them. At that moment, you are ready to make a business case for being funded.

As soon as this occurs, you can get to a PIP proposal.

Any time and money you spend on gathering information above and beyond minimal data must show cause: Is it worth more than the opportunity cost of delay in getting to a PIP?

Opportunity cost is the incremental marginal loss from money that is not invested or is not invested in a better-paying proposal.

*(text continues on page 87)*

**Figure 4-5.** Manufacturing process work flow.

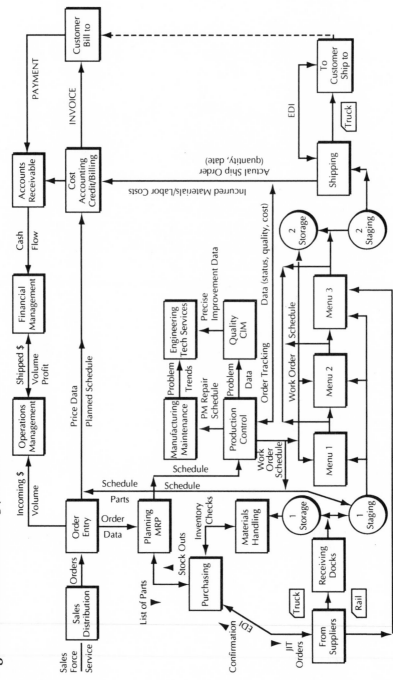

# Figure 4-6. Comparative cash flows for lease vs. buy.

## Buy

| Period | Debt Service[a] | Principal Repayment | Interest Payment | Depreciation[b] | Interest Plus Depreciation | Tax Benefit at 50 Percent | After-tax Cash Cost | Cumulative After-tax Cash Cost |
|---|---|---|---|---|---|---|---|---|
| 1 | $ 11,507 | $ 3,614 | $ 7,893 | $ 12,500 | $ 20,393 | $10,197 | $ 1,310 | $ 1,310 |
| 2 | 11,507 | 3,912 | 7,595 | 11,667 | 19,262 | 9,631 | 1,876 | 3,186 |
| 3 | 11,507 | 4,234 | 7,273 | 10,833 | 18,106 | 9,053 | 2,454 | 5,640 |
| 4 | 11,507 | 4,583 | 6,924 | 10,000 | 16,924 | 8,462 | 3,045 | 8,685 |
| 5 | 11,507 | 4,961 | 6,546 | 9,167 | 15,713 | 7,856 | 3,651 | 12,336 |
| 6 | 11,507 | 5,370 | 6,137 | 8,333 | 14,470 | 7,235 | 4,272 | 16,608 |
| 7 | 11,507 | 5,813 | 5,694 | 7,500 | 13,194 | 6,597 | 4,910 | 21,518 |
| 8 | 11,507 | 6,292 | 5,215 | 6,667 | 11,882 | 5,941 | 5,566 | 27,084 |
| 9 | 11,507 | 6,810 | 4,697 | 5,833 | 10,530 | 5,265 | 5,242 | 33,326 |
| 10 | 11,507 | 7,372 | 4,135 | 5,000 | 9,135 | 4,567 | 6,940 | 40,266 |
| 11 | 11,507 | 7,979 | 3,528 | 4,167 | 7,695 | 3,848 | 7,659 | 47,925 |
| 12 | 11,507 | 8,637 | 2,870 | 3,333 | 6,203 | 3,101 | 8,406 | 56,331 |
| 13 | 11,507 | 9,349 | 2,158 | 2,500 | 4,658 | 2,329 | 9,178 | 65,509 |
| 14 | 11,507 | 10,120 | 1,387 | 1,667 | 3,054 | 1,527 | 9,980 | 75,489 |
| 15 | 11,507 | 10,954 | 553 | 833 | 1,386 | 693 | 10,814 | 86,303 |
| | $172,605 | $100,000 | $72,605 | $100,000 | $172,605 | $86,302[d] | $86,303 | |

## Lease

| Rental[c] | Tax Benefit at 50 Percent | After-tax Cash Cost | Cumulative After-tax Cash Cost |
|---|---|---|---|
| $ 10,990 | $ 5,495 | $5,495 | $ 5,495 |
| 10,990 | 5,495 | 5,495 | 10,990 |
| 10,990 | 5,495 | 5,495 | 16,485 |
| 10,990 | 5,495 | 5,495 | 21,980 |
| 10,990 | 5,495 | 5,495 | 27,475 |
| 10,990 | 5,495 | 5,495 | 32,970 |
| 10,990 | 5,495 | 5,495 | 38,465 |
| 10,990 | 5,495 | 5,495 | 43,960 |
| 10,990 | 5,495 | 5,495 | 49,455 |
| 10,990 | 5,495 | 5,495 | 54,950 |
| 10,990 | 5,495 | 5,495 | 60,445 |
| 10,990 | 5,495 | 5,495 | 65,940 |
| 10,990 | 5,495 | 5,495 | 71,435 |
| 10,990 | 5,495 | 5,495 | 76,930 |
| 10,990 | 5,495 | 5,495 | 82,425 |
| $164,850 | $82,425 | $82,425[e] | |

NOTES

(a) $100,000 of debt borrowed at 8%. The debt service, payable quarterly in arrears, will be sufficient to amortize the loan fully over 15 years. (b) Asset cost of $100,000 will be depreciated over 15 years using the sum-of-the-years' method. It was assumed that the asset had no salvage value. (c) Rental on a 15-year lease will be payable quarterly in arrears. The rental was based on an interest factor of 7¹/₄%. It was assumed that the lessee's credit would require 8% interest. Since the lessor retains the depreciation benefits of the asset, he can charge a rent based on 7¹/₄% even though he has financed the acquisition at 8%. (d) Present worth of $86,302 cost of buying, at 8%, is $41,198. (e) Present worth of $82,425 cost of leasing, at 8%, is $47,034.

COMMENT ON NOTES (d) and (e): When comparing the cumulative after-tax cash costs, buying is the more expensive alternative by about $4,000. However, present-valuing the annual outflows results in buying's being the most economical alternative by approximately $6,000.

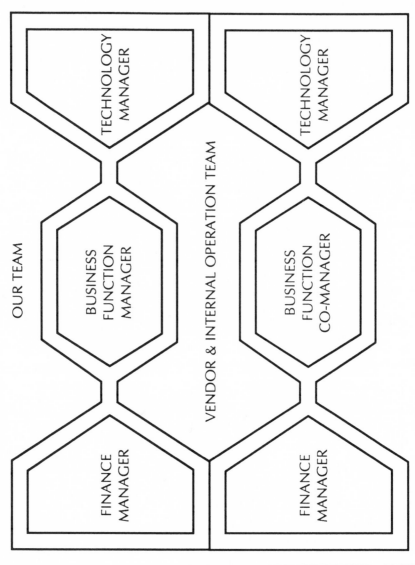

**Figure 4-7.** Joint profit-improvement team.

In other words, it is the difference in incremental profits between funding your proposal and either sitting on the money or funding someone else's. Once top management puts their money where someone else's proposal is, the funds are no longer available to put to work for you. As far as your business case is concerned, you are out of business.

A minimal data-collection system is shown in Figures 4-8 and 4-9. It composes a "fast-to-market" starter set of data that are sufficient to get you to a proposable business case. Figure 4-8 shows a quick-and-dirty assessment of cost-reduction opportunities. Figure 4-9 is its quick-and-dirty correlate for revenue-improvement opportunities. The answers in column 1 come from your money management smarts. Column 2 answers come from your skill in prescribing profit-improvement solutions. Column 3 answers come from cost-benefit analysis.

## Automating the Proposal Process

Getting to fundable PIPs fast and getting to them frequently are two of the data points that go into the hopper for calculating your

**Figure 4-8.** Cost-reduction opportunity assessment.

| Costs that we can decrease | How we can decrease them | How much in $/% we can decrease them by |
|---|---|---|
| 1. _____ | 1. _____ <br> _____ <br> _____ | 1. Avg. $_____ <br> Avg. %_____ |
| 2. _____ | 2. _____ <br> _____ <br> _____ | 2. Avg. $_____ <br> Avg. %_____ |
| 3. _____ | 3. _____ <br> _____ <br> _____ | 3. Avg. $_____ <br> Avg. %_____ |

**Figure 4-9.** Revenue-improvement opportunity assessment.

| Revenues that we can increase | How we can increase them | How much in $/% we can increase them by |
|---|---|---|
| 1. _____ | 1. _____ <br> _____ <br> _____ | 1. Avg. $_____ <br> Avg. %_____ |
| 2. _____ | 2. _____ <br> _____ <br> _____ | 2. Avg. $_____ <br> Avg. %_____ |
| 3. _____ | 3. _____ <br> _____ <br> _____ | 3. Avg. $_____ <br> Avg. %_____ |

reliability as a profit improver. Both of these criteria can be met with a much higher level of confidence when the proposal process is automated.

Automation confers three benefits on the preparation and presentation of your PIPs:

1. It permits you to generate a steady state of proposals, enabling you to make a more continuous impact on management's profits by acting in a perpetual proposal mode without taking unwarranted amounts of time away from running your day-to-day operations.
2. It makes it easy for your proposals to conform to top management's comfort levels of accuracy, giving you the security of knowing that the arithmetic of profit improvement is always correct, whether or not you are a "numbers person."
3. It lets you concentrate your time and talent on the creative areas of profit-improvement strategy and not fritter them away on the mechanics of the proposal process.

Mack Hanan's FundMaster™—nicknamed "The Business Case on a Disk"—is a software program that prepares proposals that are professional-class value propositions. FundMaster lets you diagnose a business problem or opportunity that fits a management strategic objective, analyzes the costs and benefits of as many "What-if" optional solutions you can generate, calculates the cash flow, net profit improvement, payback and rate of return on investment from the single best solution you select to propose, and specifies the revised operations and workflows that are required to achieve them.

FundMaster previews for your top managers the most likely outcomes from funding your proposals: how much cost you can reduce, how much new revenue you can contribute to, and how soon you can do it. It provides the data for answers to the critical few questions that stand between every proposal and its close: How will our profits be improved? By how much? How soon? At what rate of return? At what risk?

Figure 4-10 shows how a FundMaster cost-benefit analysis looks as it scrolls across a computer screen.

When management wants to see alternatives, or wants to know which ones you have considered before coming up with your single best recommendation, automation like FundMaster allows you to generate endless variations of your proposals in microseconds just by changing a single entry:

- What does a lower investment buy us?
- How can we move up payback?
- What does the return look like if the investment is cycled over several years instead of being front-end loaded?
- What if we lease these assets instead of purchasing them?

As management's questions get answered in real time, their natural propensity to postpone making the decision to go ahead is progressively discouraged. Why wait? If there are no more questions to ask and there are no reasons not to go ahead and no better uses for the money on the table right now, when can we get

*(text continues on page 93)*

™FundMaster by PIPWARE™ is a registered trademark of Mack Hanan.

**Figure 4-10.** Automatic cost-benefit analysis.

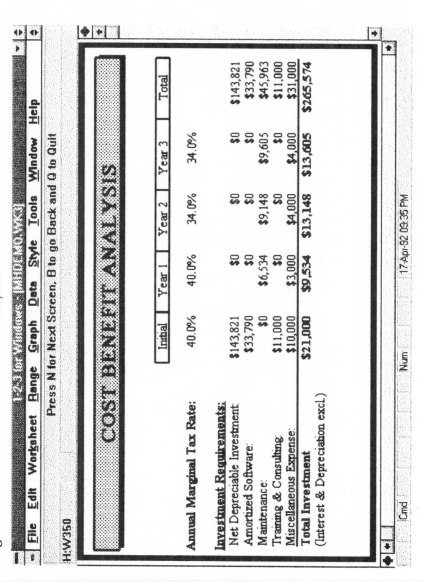

File  Edit  Worksheet  Range  Graph  Data  Style  Tools  Window  Help

H:W350

# COST BENEFIT ANALYSIS, Continued

|  | Initial | Year 1 | Year 2 | Year 3 | Total |
|---|---|---|---|---|---|
| **Anticipated Profit Contribution Due to:** | | | | | |
| Cost Avoidances (Internal Staff) | | $160,000 | $336,000 | $528,000 | $2,147,483 |
| Cost Reductions (Accellerated Invoicing) | | $22,000 | $22,000 | $22,000 | $110,000 |
| TOTAL: | | $182,000 | $358,000 | $550,000 | $2,257,483 |
| **Pro Forma Profit Improvement (Net Change)** | | | | | |
| Gross Profit Improvement: | ($21,000) | $172,466 | $344,852 | $536,395 | $2,169,520 |
| Less: Depreciation Expense | N.A. | $35,522 | $35,522 | $35,522 | $177,611 |
| Profit Improvement before Int + Ta | ($21,000) | $136,944 | $309,330 | $500,872 | $1,991,909 |
| Interest Expense: | N.A. | $0 | $0 | $0 | $0 |
| Profit Improvement Before Taxes: | ($21,000) | $136,944 | $309,330 | $500,872 | $1,991,909 |
| Tax Expenses: | ($8,400) | $54,778 | $105,172 | $170,297 | $684,206 |
| Net Profit Improvement: | ($12,600) | $82,166 | $204,158 | $330,576 | $1,307,703 |

Cmd          Num          17-Apr-92 09:35 PM

(continues)

**Figure 4-10.** (continued)

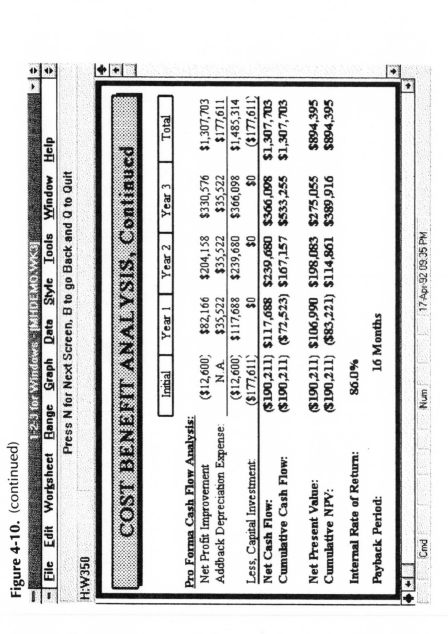

File  Edit  Worksheet  Range  Graph  Data  Style  Tools  Window  Help

Press N for Next Screen, B to go Back and Q to Quit

H:W350

## COST BENEFIT ANALYSIS, Continued

|  | Initial | Year 1 | Year 2 | Year 3 | Total |
|---|---|---|---|---|---|
| **Pro Forma Cash Flow Analysis:** | | | | | |
| Net Profit Improvement | ($12,600) | $82,166 | $204,158 | $330,576 | $1,307,703 |
| Addback Depreciation Expense: | N.A. | $35,522 | $35,522 | $35,522 | $177,611 |
|  | ($12,600) | $117,688 | $239,680 | $366,098 | $1,485,314 |
| Less, Capital Investment: | ($177,611) | $0 | $0 | $0 | ($177,611) |
| **Net Cash Flow:** | **($190,211)** | **$117,688** | **$239,680** | **$366,098** | **$1,307,703** |
| **Cumulative Cash Flow:** | **($190,211)** | **($72,523)** | **$167,157** | **$533,255** | **$1,307,703** |
| **Net Present Value:** | **($190,211)** | **$106,990** | **$198,083** | **$275,055** | **$894,395** |
| **Cumulative NPV:** | **($190,211)** | **($83,221)** | **$114,861** | **$389,916** | **$894,395** |
| **Internal Rate of Return:** | 86.0% | | | | |
| **Payback Period:** | 16 Months | | | | |

Cmd          Num          17-Apr-92 09:35 PM

started? In this way, your cycle time for getting funded can be significantly compressed.

This can help you acquire more funds over each operating period. It also frees up top management to make more deals faster with you and other managers by reducing each deal's approval time.

Automated proposals change the substance of management's concern. They no longer need to "worry the numbers" to see if they add up. They can focus on using their own strengths to see how they can make your numbers come out better. Instead of forcing top managers into playing the negative role of auditors, you can partner with them as fellow strategists so that they work with you, not against you, to prove that they can help you do better rather than try to prove you wrong.

This will encourage you to be more of a perpertual as well as a high-percentage performer who turns out one fundable proposal and one money-making profit-improvement project after another. As a result, you will be more likely to get first dibs when budgets are being handed out.

Making partner with top management is based on performing within your promises. When management puts their money on you, they are making you a dedicated supplier of the funds they expect you to return on their investment. You are the sole provider. If you fail to deliver the goods, management suffers a shortfall. Unless it can be made up by a manager of another operation, there will be less money in the corporate kitty for the next round of budgeting.

By returning management's investments in your profit-improvement projects on time and generating positive cash flows from them that create new values, you become accountable for your partner's success—that is, as a source of funds, you become the equivalent of a customer account. This is the role reversal you must accomplish with your upstairs bankers in order to get funded.

As soon as top managers sign off on one of your requests for appropriation, you become at risk. So do they. This commonality of risk partners you, joining you inseparably at the wallet. Without shared risk, where management is the lender and you are the multiplier of borrowed funds, partnership cannot exist.

This is why top managers are in the market for only one kind of partner: business partners, not operations partners or function partners or technical partners. Business partners have the single, transcendent characteristic of contributing to improved profitability. They do not cost money; they generate money. They help grow the business, which is the stuff of which business partnerships are made.

What do top managers want from a partnership with you? They want added power and prestige. They want added money income. They want added achievement, which translates into added psychic income from achieving competitive leadership. They want added control, to keep in charge of their own destiny. In business, either you are in control or you are out of control. If you are out of control, you are going to be out of business.

If you are a Chrysler manager and you want to partner with Chairman Bob Eaton, you must add to his "short-term, quantifiable results" from being funded.

If you are a Unisys manager and you want to partner with Chairman Jim Unruh, you must add to his "tangible, bottom-line results."

If you are a Quaker Oats manager and you want to partner with CEO Bill Smithburg, you must add to his portfolio of projects that "deliver cash flows that exceed the cash required to pay for them."

If you are a manager at American Home Products, and you want to partner with Chairman John Stafford, you must add more benefits than costs. He will "call you in for lunch" if your expenditures go over the funds you are budgeted for. No one gets invited to lunch twice.

If you are a manager at Procter & Gamble and you want to partner with Chairman Ed Artzt, you must add to his profits. He stalks the floors of P & G to find people who misuse his funds to produce numbers he doesn't like. And when he finds them, he has one message for them: "Get results or I'll clear you out and sell the business."

# 5

# Operating as a Virtual Business

A virtual corporation is a temporary confederation of autonomous businesses. Each business brings to the party a core capability that the others require to serve a specific market need: a technical expertise, a distribution channel, or sales skills. A truer definition would be "virtual unincorporation," since nobody owns anybody else. When the needs that bring them together have been served, the parts are disassembled and put together again in different combinations as other virtual organizations.

Virtuality is a way for top management to have their cake and eat it, too—to have the use of assets they want only when they want them without being saddled with their development, maintenance, innovation, or reengineering costs. The only thing that management pays for is usage.

Virtual operations come close to the ideal of zero assets under ownership. In practice, each company's management ends up owning only its own strategic businesses and their core capabilities while joint venturing, leasing, and outsourcing everything else that is nonstrategic.

Outsourcing a capability removes its assets from the corporate balance sheet and reduces its cost of ownership to zero. You can accomplish the same result by running your operation as a net contributor of profits to management so that you become a *virtual outsourcer* by accounting for zero operating costs.

Managing "as if"—as if your operation were an outsource—is the conceptual framework for managing a cost center as a profit contributor. It is also the requisite mind-set for remaining an insource. Any capability that cannot be cost-competitive with the average performance standards of its industry benchmarks is an unaffordable luxury. Letting somebody else manage it from the outside whose benchmarks exceed the industry average is the preferred solution.

## Operating With Make-Believe Autonomy

In order to be a virtual outsourcer, you must be able to replicate an outsourcer's basic value proposition by returning more than you cost. On a project-by-project basis, this is what each of your business cases must be designed to do. Cumulatively, each year's portfolio of your business cases must be able to yield an average net dollar value and a rate of return equal to or better than the combined average of the best outsourcers.

"Insource profits or see your operations outsourced" is a good caveat to keep in mind as a basic business principle. It will remind you that your true competitors are professional money managers, not your peers who are operating managers, when it comes to benchmarking your operation's financial performance. To be competitive with money managers, you must match them on a costs-and-benefits basis, proposal by proposal.

If you envision yourself as managing an autonomous business instead of a business function—as if you are an independent product developer if you are an R & D manager, a contract manufacturer if you are a process manager, or a business development consultant if you are a sales or marketing manager—you will ask yourself each time you propose why your top managers will prefer to do business with you. The answer will no longer be because they own you. Your only recourse is to propose the same type of competitive business cases, with the same type of competitive profit-improvement proposals, that all outsiders must present to get business—that is, to get funded.

Coming at your top managers as if you were coming from the outside, yet still retaining the insider's competitive advantage of unlimited access to your key people and their key data, will open your eyes to many things:

- Where your work flows are larded over with too many inefficiencies for you to be a low-cost supplier.

- Where their cycle times are too slow for you to excel in being first-to-market or in delivering inventory on a JIT basis.
- Where your quality standards and productivity schedules are incompatible with each other and create conflict between satisfying your internal constituents and your external customers.
- Where your applications smarts need to be beefed up to the level of your processing smarts.

You will also see immediately that, despite being on the inside track, you have probably been remiss in learning top management's business objectives and the business strategies they have planned to realize them. It will give you small comfort to realize that your top management's business strategies are the first thing an outsourcer targets, starting with learning what they are and going on to fitting his value propositions into them.

Managing your operation "as if" you are autonomous makes you appreciate why it is no longer adequate to be a responsive, reactive supplier who listens to your internal customers, takes your direction from them and is driven by their needs. With an outsources's mind-set, it will be second nature for you to take leadership in stretching customer objectives, either helping to enlarge them or to condense the time required for their realization. If you sit back and wait to react, you will always be working toward benchmarks that have already been accepted as industry standards, rather than reaching out to be first to own the next standards that will supersede them.

Falling behind a standards curve is catastrophic. But hanging on to the fat part of the curve hand-over-hand with your competitors is merely to be a commodity supplier. Getting to the next curve first and getting off it first onto the next curve after that is taking *leadership*—not simply in your operating technology but also in its contributions to profits.

## Managing Profit-Improvement Projects

Think of profit-improvement projects as if they are your products. You are their manufacturer, turning them out under Total Quality

Management (TQM) on a just-in-time (JIT) basis with maximum productivity consistent with quality that is acceptable at the standards of customer satisfaction set by your funders.

You always want to have profit-improvement projects in your pipeline. Unless you maintain a steady state of sales upstairs, you will incur opportunity costs from not being funded. Downtime or returned goods—projects whose proposals get bounced—are costly interruptions. They make your state of supply unsteady. Their ultimate cost is the window they may open for the funding of your competitors' projects—that is, for competitive projects to be sold upstairs by other managers while you are out of the market.

Think of yourself as a sales manager and your project team managers as your sales force. How high is your close rate? How short is your sales cycle? How consistent is customer satisfaction?

This is the proper vision for operating a virtual business, where your lifeblood is how good you are at generating and managing projects to improve top management's profitability.

Project management has five rules:

1. Each project must have a single objective on which its success can be measured. Secondary objectives are bonuses.
2. A project must be managed so that its objective can be achieved at minimal investment with minimal resources in minimal time.
3. A project must turn over as quickly as possible so that its management resources can be recycled.
4. The number of projects under management should fully capitalize resources. Too few projects undercapitalize resources. Too many projects outrun the supply of good managers and may dissipate funds.
5. Projects should be sequenced according to the priority of their objectives and to maximize benefits from synergy.

Managing a profit-improvement project is a multistep process. You select the project, its manager, and team; create the project plan and analyze its profit contribution and risks; and decide either to go or not to go ahead. Figure 5-1 shows this step-by-step process.

**Figure 5-1.** Project management process.

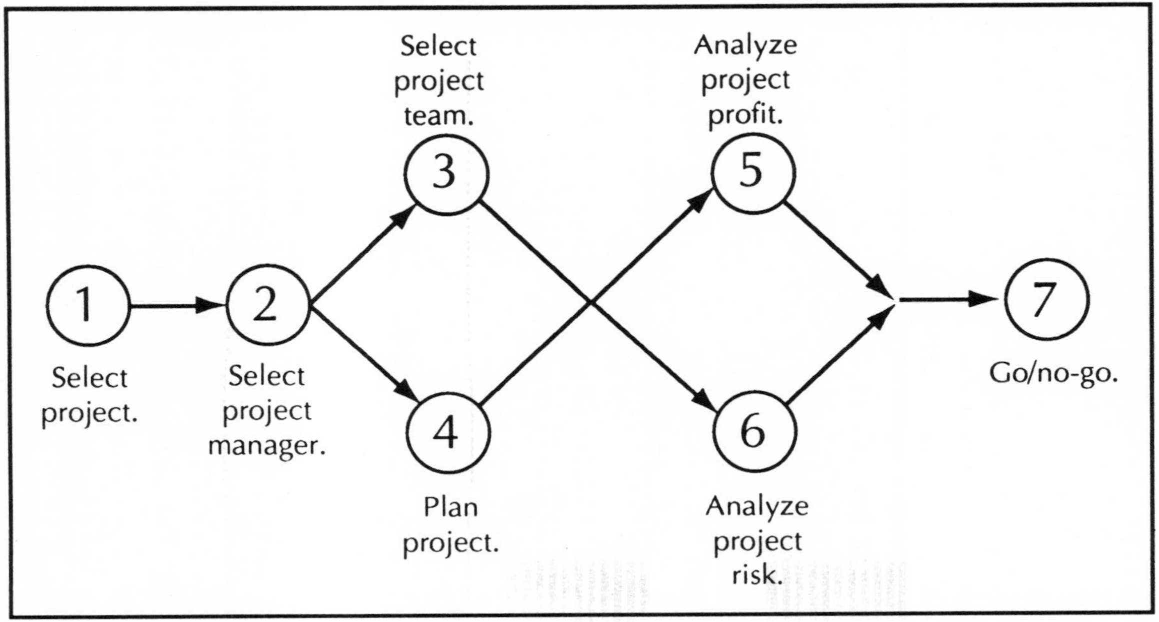

## Select the Project

You should always have an inventory of potential projects "on the shelf." Two criteria qualify a project for inventory:

1. It must be able to yield a rate of return on the resources required to be invested in it that is equal to or exceeds the minimum hurdle rate for incremental corporate investments.
2. It must have a consistent fit with corporate strategic business objectives by contributing to the achievement of "must needs."

You need a different set of criteria for selecting the rank order of projects to take out of inventory. Financially speaking, a project with the best net present value contribution is generally a preferred investment. Net present value (NPV) permits you to make direct comparisons of competing investments because it sums up each project's total value after all its outlays have been subtracted and the time value of money has been factored in. In order to make NPV even more selective, you can apply three criteria to it:

1. *Annual cash flows on a year-by-year basis.* This shows how a project builds progressive value, at what rate, and for how long.
2. *Payback period.* This shows how long a project's initial negative cash flow persists, when its investment can be recovered to plow back into reinvestment, and how long it takes for a project to become self-capitalizing.
3. *Proceeds per unit outlay.* This shows the continuity and duration of a project's cash flows after payback so that the total proceeds over the project's life from each dollar of outlay can be calculated.

Financial criteria can be "smoothed" by applying operating considerations such as these:

- *Probability of success.* This attempts to evaluate the likelihood of achieving a project's planned objectives.

- *Positive follow-on impact.* This attempts to evaluate the likelihood of a project leading to future benefits.
- *Readiness to go.* This attempts to evaluate the likelihood of a project proceeding at once from current capabilities that do not require significant renovation or costly and unproven innovation.
- *Key people intensivity.* This attempts to evaluate the likelihood of tying up key people in a project for so long a time that unaffordable opportunity cost is incurred on future projects.

## Select the Manager

A project manager owns the project. He or she is its chief executive officer, the author of its plan, and the selector of its team. The standard of performance for a project manager is met when the project is managed as a profit center so that it achieves its planned objective on budget and on time.

Project management is a Type A job. Type A traits and characteristics define a manager in the following ways:

- Good at problem definition and solution
- Personal identification with a project as "my project"
- Persuasive leadership style that relies on personal decision making following participative consultation rather than consensus
- Dedication to seeing things through to completion
- Distaste for ambiguity
- Compulsively time-driven and deadline-oriented
- Highly competitive and going all-out
- Multiphasic ability to do several things at once
- High personal standards of performance that must be met
- Ambition to succeed and fear of failure
- Bias against bureaucracy, rules, and tradition
- Preference to deal directly and informally to get results

## Select the Team

A model project team consists of between three and six principal players, following the minimal-team model shown in Figure 4-7.

The project team is a center of competence. Its competence must be project-specific, providing it with exactly the right capability mix to achieve the project's objective. Morton's Rule must always apply: The team must "sit in the same room" and report to the same leader according to the same standards of performance and shared rewards.

## Plan the Project

Each project should be planned from its objective backwards and from its "customer" inwards.

In the case of an operating project, the customer is a line of business manager or another business function manager. The project's flow should be planned like this:

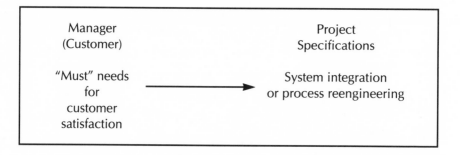

For control, each project should be divided into a small number of major tasks. Each task should be planned separately on a single sheet of paper according to its sequential rank order in the project's critical path. Figure 5-2 shows a narrative version of a critical-path sequence. Its visualization is shown in Figure 5-3.

## Analyze Profit and Risk

A project's opportunity to contribute profits must be balanced against its risk of not contributing them—or of not contributing as much profit as planned or not contributing it on time.

Risk analysis is an attempt to convert the uncertainty about these risks into probability by measuring it on a subjective scale of likelihood. It requires comparative bets like these:

**Figure 5-2.** Critical-path narrative.

| Task | Est. Time Days | Precede by | Follow by |
|------|----------------|------------|-----------|
| A | 4 | | B,C,G |
| B | 3 | A | D |
| C | 2 | A | E |
| D | 4 | B | F |
| E | 1 | C | F |
| F | 4 | D,E | H |
| G | 6 | A | H |
| H | 1 | F,G | J |
| I | 1 | H | |

**Figure 5-3.** Critical-path visualization.

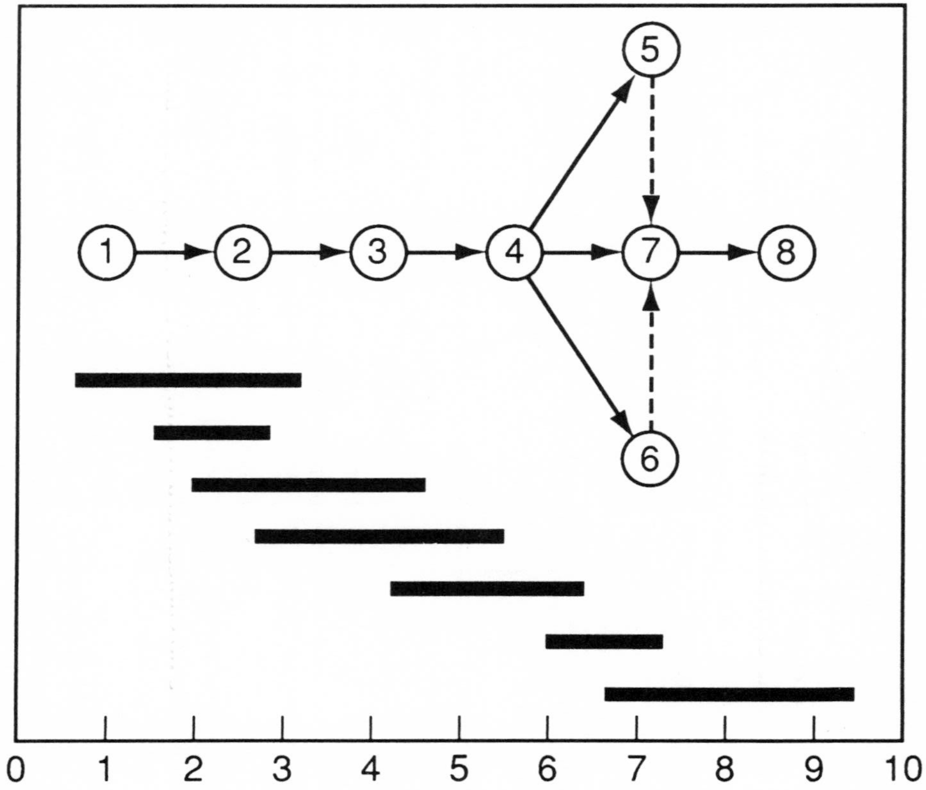

- What is the amount of probable impact on a project's proposed added value by foreseeable future events?
- What is the probable likelihood of each event?

Risk can be further assessed by asking questions like these:

- What is the chance of this event happening? One in nine? One in five?
- If it happens, what is the chance it can make a 90 percent change in my objectives? One in nine? One in five? What is the chance it can make a 50 percent change?

## Benchmarking to Outsourcer's Standards

If you were to be spun out as a freestanding, autonomous business, from the morning of day 1 you would have to manage your operation to meet two standards of performance:

1. To be self-supporting in *your business income,* since you would be cut off from corporate sponsorship for your source of funds.
2. To be able to improve the profits of your customers by continuous enhancement of *their business outcomes* so they can generate the funds to retain you over and over again.

True outsourcers manage to these dual standards every day. They have no choice. As a result, they can engage your top managers in proposals like this:

> We are experts in the continuous improvement of the contribution to profits made by order entry with electronic data interchange (EDI) [or product development or inventory management or same-day order fulfillment]. Our experience proves that we can normally reduce this operation's contribution to cost by a minimum of 15 percent in year one [or improve this function's contribution to revenues by a minimum of 15 percent over a three-year time frame] as co-managers with your in-

house management team. We will guarantee this minimum contribution, which will give you such-and-such a
rate of return on your start-up investment.

If we are able to exceed our minimum guarantee, we
will gainshare with you at the rate of 20 to 30 cents on
each incremental dollar saved or earned.

Outsourcers' standards must become your standards. In every
industry, outsourcers are setting your industry's standard outcomes. Unless you can adhere to them, top management will flow
their funds to the source of the best returns. Whether that is outside or inside may not make a difference if the difference in return
is significant.

Paul Strassmann, formerly Xerox chief information officer
(CIO), sees the handwriting on the wall for information technology
managers in deals like Xerox outsourcing its data center operations
to Electronic Data Systems (EDS) and Kodak doing the same with
IBM and Digital Equipment. "For the past decade, CIOs have been
diddling around as strategists instead of sticking to their knitting."
As business managers take control of information budgets, "the
guys who look at the bottom line will outsource."

The way to achieve outsourcer standards is to take ownership
of their ten basic strategies: to implement them; to institutionalize
them through training and a system of rewards and punishments,
and the measurement of results; and to commit your management
team to their fulfillment.

1. *Visualize your operation through your funders' eyes.* Imagine
that your top managers are your customers. If they could design
your operation from the ground up for partnership with them—
think of "design for partnership" as a correlate of "design for manufacturing"—what would it look like? How would it be organized?
How would it operate? What performance standards would make
it management's first choice as their business partner?

2. *Set stretch objectives* for the minimum number of standards
required to establish satisfaction with your management customers. You must be one of the lowest-cost producers. Comparative
low cost is necessary; absolute lowest cost is not. But you must be
one of the highest consistent profit improvers. This is more the

result of the quality of applications skills of your people's intellectual assets—how adept they are at managing profit-improvement projects—than your operation's capital assets.

3. *Do more with less.* Maximize your productivity per headcount and minimize the overhead required to maintain a steady state of innovation. The more work you get out of each dollar, the more dollars you can get to put to work. Become famous for your ability to make a little go a long way. Eschew building an internal empire. Build profits instead.

4. *Map your processes.* Continuously improve your work flows and their cycle times. Integrate and reintegrate their systems, creating new configurations by combining some while eliminating or outsourcing others for continuously improved cost-effectiveness. Apply the workout principle to make every process justify itself.

5. *Benchmark best practices.* Make your industry standards your baseline, not your goal line. Concentrate on coming as close as possible to being best of breed in comparison with outsourcer standards, which means that you must achieve parity with the best of them and inferiority to none.

6. *Empower decision making down to the lowest levels.* Getting things done for the sake of getting things done is good management practice whenever being first earns funding. Train your people to aim-ready-fire: *aim* at profit-improvement opportunities fast, get *ready* to propose them fast, and *fire* fast before they incur opportunity cost. Getting to an opportunity last may turn out to be the same as not getting there at all.

7. *Gainshare in your results.* Make a deal with management to base your funding on the value of the gains you create so that you can share in them as a business partner. Get agreement on a ratio of fundable dollars per dollars of return on a project-by-project basis so that your funds are acknowledged to be the result—and not seen as the cost—of your performance.

8. *Free the flow of information* so that everyone in your operation can come up with leads for profit-improvement projects. Spread the word on work flow costs and cycle times. Make everyone aware of the contributions your operation can make to improved productivity and quality in other operations and to improved revenues in the lines of business you support. Position

the free flow of information as a right that carries with it the responsibility to apply it to create profit-improvement projects on the basis of "use it or lose access to it."

9. *Endorse a common vision* of your operating role as contributing financial benefits to management as well as performance benefits to their business lines. Attach price tags to your work flows and cycle times to publicize their contributions to costs. Assign dollar values from potential savings and revenue gains by improving work flows and cycle times at the power of one percent. Get everybody "What if-ing" profit-improvement proposals. Redefine your mission in terms of contributing minimal costs to revenue generation, putting the focus on the cash flows you help to turn over rather than the products or services you help to turn out.

10. *Bring in the customer*. Make top management's "customer satisfaction" your operation's driving force. In this way everything you do will fit a strategic business objective and satisfy one or more of the critical success factors for its competitive advantage.

# Appendixes

# Appendix A

# How Top Managers Budget for Capital Expenditures

Top managers plan and evaluate their expenditures to acquire capital assets by a method known as the capital budgeting process. It consists of four steps:

1. Project planning
2. Outcome evaluation
3. Cash control
4. Postaudit evaluation

The first step in capital budgeting proceeds on the assumption that a company has a formal long-range plan or, at the least, the proposed project fits into the mainstream of the corporation's interest. Implicit in a proposal is a forecast of markets, revenues, costs, expenses, profit. These aspects of capital budgeting are the most important, most time-consuming, most critical phase, and largely outside of the area of expertise of the financial executive. A major project generally affects marketing, engineering, manufacturing, and finance.

The uncertainties surrounding a long-range forecast are often great enough to throw doubt on the effectiveness of the entire decision-making process. Probability analysis of success/failure becomes important in view of the uncertainties. A relatively simple approach to evaluating uncertainty is discussed later. However, sophisticated probability analysis and computer simulation can be

From Mack Hanan, *Consultative Selling*™ (New York: AMACOM, 1991), adapted from "The Capital Budgeting Process," a monograph by Coopers & Lybrand, 1973, and reprinted by permission.

beneficial in giving credibility to major long-range projections in the face of great uncertainty. Unless this phase of capital budgeting is made reliable and meaningful, the decision-making phase simply becomes an exercise in arithmetic.

The second stage, project evaluation and decision-making methods, has received major attention in accounting and financial publications. There is general agreement that the time-adjusted cash-flow methods (net present value and discounted cash flow [DCF] rate of return) are most meaningful guides to the investment decision; however, there is still place for cash payback analysis in appraising the financial risks inherent in a projection. These methods will be examined and brought into perspective for use in the proposed model. Within certain limits, and they can be identified, these measures will give the best tools for appraising proposals. They do not produce the magic "go/no-go" answer. They give management guidance. No matter what quantitative guidlines are developed, qualitative factors will be important in the final decision; the personal judgments and preferences of the project sponsor and management cannot be discounted.

The third step, control and audit of cash, is the simplest step in the budgeting process once the source of funds has been determined and committed. After approval, the project should be treated as any other budgeted item, with payment schedules determined and variances reported and explained. Major overspending can impair the validity of the investment decision, and even invalidate the entire process.

A caution is appropriate at this point. When a proposal calls for a specific investment, it is implicit that no more than that amount will be spent. Overspending of any significant amount cannot be permitted. Similarly, a project sponsor should not come back the next year for additional funds because he underestimated his original request. When either of these events occurs, it becomes necessary to refigure the entire project on the total cash outlay. Unfortunately, at this point the company is already irrevocably committed to the project, and the new calculations are after the fact.

The fourth step, post-audit evaluating and reporting of results of investment, is a task that everyone agrees needs doing, but is rarely done. As will be reviewed below, capital investments are projected on an incremental basis, on a cash basis, and on an internal rate of return basis over the life of the investment. Regular financial records and reports are on an annual basis, on an accrual basis, or on a rate of return by individual years. A major problem is that many projects become an integral part of a larger, existing investment and the new project cannot be separated from the existing one. The postaudit of the incremental segment may become obscure or meaningless. As a result, many incremental investments cannot be appraised against objectives, for example, a large rate of return. The large projected incremental rate of return may become diluted when merged with a larger investment. There may be general disappointment because the new investment results have not lived up to forecasts and, yet, the projected earnings and cash flow of the incremental investment may be right on target. New criteria for postaudit may have to be determined to affect postaudit for many projects at the time the original projections are made so that management knows how it will measure results against plan. One criterion may be cash flow. Another criterion may be the development of pro forma statements comparing financial income before and after the additional investment, that is, a financial model. The main point is that good budgeting calls for comparisons of projections and results, and though the project evaluation criteria may not be susceptible to audit in many cases, it should not preclude the establishment of other criteria for postaudit purposes at the time the original projection is made. The use of pro forma statements indicating total results as well as impact on earnings per share before and after the investment may be the appropriate basis for appraisal of the additional investment.

## Principles of Capital Investment Analysis

This section describes the specific concepts used to evaluate major capital expenditure projects and programs within the scope of the capital budgeting process. The underlying concepts and methods used are examined to bring into focus the economic consequences of a capital expenditure.

When a capital expenditure is proposed, the project must be evaluated and the economic consequences of the commitment of funds determined before referring it to a budget committee for review or to management for approval. How are the economic consequences described best? This is done in two steps:

First, set up the project into a standard economic model that can be used for all projects no matter how dissimilar to each other they may be.

$$\text{Benefits} - \text{costs} = \text{cash flow}$$

To describe the formula in accounting terminology:

| | |
|---|---|
| *Benefits:* | Projected cash revenue from sales and other sources |
| *Costs:* | Nonrecurring cash outlays for assets, plus recurring operating expenses |
| *Cash flow:* | Net income after taxes plus noncash charges for such items as depreciation |

Thus, if the model were stated in a conventional accounting form it would appear as:

| | |
|---|---|
| *Add:* | Cash revenues projected (benefits) |
| *Less:* | Cash investment outlay and cash expenses (costs) |
| *Total:* | Cash flow |

The "benefits less costs" model is usually developed within the framework of the company's accounts and supported with prescribed supplementary schedules that show the basis of the projection.

It should be apparent that in setting up an economic model, the conventional accrual accounting concept, net income after taxes, has been abandoned. The established criterion is cash flow—new income after tax plus noncash charges.

Second, adjust the cash flow into relevant financial terms. The cash flow projected for each year over the life of the proposal has to be translated into financial terms that are valid; that is, translate the annual dollar cash flows to a common dollar value in a base year. This concept must not be confused with attempts to adjust for changes in the purchasing power of the dollar.

The calculations assume no significant erosion in the purchasing power of the dollar. Should this occur, the time-adjusted common dollar concept may require adjustments for the diminished real value (purchasing power) of future dollar payments. The common dollar value concept used in capital budgeting adjusts for time value only. This is achieved through the development of the concept of discounting and present value that will be examined in the next section. An examination of how a simple two-step model is developed will illustrate the rationale of this approach.

In the first step we set up the economic model: Benefits minus costs equals cash flow. To complete this model, we need to identify in detail all economic benefits and costs associated with the project. Benefits typically take the form of sales revenues and other income. Costs normally include nonrecurring outlays for fixed assets, investments in working capital, and recurring outlays for payrolls, materials, and expenses.

For each element of benefits and costs that the project involves, we forecast the amount of change for each year. How far ahead do we forecast? For as long as the expenditure decision will continue to have effects: that is, for as long as they generate costs and significant benefits. Forecasts are made for each year of the project's life; we call the year of decision "year 0," the next year "year 1," and so on. When the decision's effects extend so far into the future that estimates are very conjectural, the model stops forecasting at a "planning horizon" (ten to fifteen years), far enough in the future to establish clearly whether the basis for the decision is a correct one.

We apply a single economic concept in forecasting costs: opportunity cost. The opportunity cost of a resource (asset) is what the company loses from not using it in an alternative way or exchanging it for another asset. For example, if cash has earning power of 15 percent after taxes, we speak of the cash as having an opportunity cost of 15 percent. Whenever an asset is acquired for a cash payment, the opportunity cost is, of course, the cash given up to acquire it. It is harder to establish the opportunity cost of committing assets already owned or controlled. If owned land committed to a project would otherwise be sold, the opportunity cost is the after-tax proceeds from the sale. The opportunity cost of using productive equipment, transportation vehicles, or plant facilities is the incremental profit lost because these resources are unavailable for other purposes. If the alternative to using owned facilities is idleness, the opportunity cost is zero. Although opportunity costs are difficult to identify and measure, they must be considered if we are to describe the economic consequences of a decision as accurately as possible. An understanding of this concept of opportunity cost is probably the most critical to this economic analysis and is generally quite foreign to the manager.

At the end of the first step, we have an economic model for the project's life showing forecast cash flows for each year. In the second step we convert the results into financial terms that are meaningful for decision making. We must take into account the one measurable financial effect of an investment decision left out in step 1: time. Dollars shown in different years of the model cannot be compared since time makes them of dissimilar value. We clearly recognize that if we have an opportunity to invest funds and earn 15 percent a year and we have a choice of receiving $1,000 today or a year from now, we will take the $1,000 today, so that it can be invested and earn $150. On this basis $1,000 available a year from now is worth less than $1,000 today. It is this adjustment for time that is required to make cash flows in different years comparable; that is, discounting.

This time value of funds available for investment is known as the opportunity cost of capital. This should not be confused with the cost of raising capital—debt or equity—or with the company's average earnings rate. Like the opportunity cost of any resource, the opportunity cost of capital is what it will cost the company to use capital for an investment project in terms of what this capital could earn elsewhere.

The opportunity cost of capital is alternatively referred to as the minimum acceptable rate of interest, the marginal rate of interest, the minimum rate of return, the marginal rate of return, and the cost of capital. Whatever the term used, and they are used loosely and interchangeably, it reflects the rate the corporation decides it can be reasonably sure of getting by using the money in another way. It is developed through the joint efforts of management, which identifies relevant opportunities, and the controller, who translates management's judgment into a marginal rate.

Another simple economic concept must be introduced: incremental cost, sometimes called differential cost or marginal cost. By definition, it is the change in cost (or revenue) that results from a decision to expand or contract an operation. It is the difference in total cost. In performing the capital budgeting analysis, we deal with incremental costs (revenues) only. Sunk or existing costs are not relevant to the evaluation and decision.

Throughout this study all references to costs and revenues are on an incremental basis.

## Rationale of Discounting and Present Value

Discounting is a technique used to find the value today or "present value" of money paid or received in the future. This value is found from the following formula:

Future dollar amount × discount factor = present value

The discount factor depends on the opportunity cost of capital expressed as an interest rate and a time period. Figure A-1 illustrates how discount factors are usually displayed. The discount factors are grouped according to the annual interest rate, expressed as the present value of $1, and then listed according to the year the amount comes due. The table should be read this way: When a dollar earns 10 percent per year uniformly over time, a dollar received at the end of the second year is equivalent to (worth) about 86 cents today.

**Figure A-1.** Present value of $1 at 10 percent.

| Year | Present Value (Today's Value) |
|------|-------------------------------|
| 0–1  | $0.9516                       |
| 1–2  | 0.8611                        |
| 2–3  | 0.7791                        |
| 3–4  | 0.7050                        |
| 4–5  | 0.6379                        |

# Arithmetic and Concept of Present Value

To adjust the model's results for the time element, we "discount" both the positive and negative cash flow forecasts for each period at the company's marginal rate of return to determine their present value. This discounting process makes the forecasts equivalent in time. We can now add the present values of these cash flow forecasts to derive the net present value (NPV). The NPV is a meaningful measure of the economic consequences of an investment decision since it measures all benefits and all costs, including the opportunity cost of capital.

When the net present value of a proposed investment is determined, we are ready to decide whether it should be accepted. This is done by comparing it to the economic consequences of doing nothing or of accepting an alternative. The general rule followed in comparing alternative projects is to choose the course of action that results in the highest net present value.

Figure A-2 illustrates the cash flow forecasts and time-value calculations for a typical proposal to invest in a new project when the alternative is to do nothing, that is, maintain liquidity rather than invest. A discount rate of 10 percent is assumed as the company's marginal rate.

The proposed project will cost $500 in year 0, and cash operating expenses thereafter will be $200 per year for four years. Assume the cash benefits will be positive but decline over the four years and total $1,450. The cash flow is negative in the year of

**Figure A-2.** Arithmetic of determining net present value (NPV).

| Year | Benefits | Costs | Cash Flow | PV of $1 @ 10% | Discounted Cash Flow |
|------|----------|-------|-----------|----------------|---------------------|
| 0 | $ 0 | $ (500) | $(500) | 1.000 | $(500) |
| 0–1 | 425 | (200) | 225 | .952 | 214 |
| 1–2 | 425 | (200) | 225 | .861 | 194 |
| 2–3 | 350 | (200) | 150 | .779 | 117 |
| 3–4 | 250 | (200) | 50 | .705 | 35 |
| TOTAL | $1,450 | $(1,300) | $ 150 | | $ 60 NPV |

investment but positive in the succeeding years, and there is a net positive cash flow over the life of the project of $150 before discounting. When the cash flow forecasts are made equivalent in time by multiplying each annual cash flow by the present value of the dollar for each period, the time-adjusted cash flow is determined, and the net present value is found to be $60. The proposed investment is better than doing nothing because all costs are covered, the 10 percent opportunity cost of the corporation's funds is realized, and in addition, the project will yield an additional $60 return.

Figure A-2 indicates an NPV of $60. Depending on the cash flow and/or the discount rate, the NPV could be negative or zero. If the NPV were zero, the company would have projected earnings exactly equal to its marginal rate of 10 percent. If there were no alternative projects, and the only alternative were to do nothing, the project with the NPV of zero would be accepted because the company would earn its marginal rate of return. (As explained later, the NPV of zero would yield the discounted cash flow rate of return, that is, 10 percent.) If the NPV were negative because of an inadequate cash flow, assuming the same 10 percent marginal rate required by management, it would mean the project would earn less than 10 percent, and it would be rejected.

There are a number of evaluation methods that are employed in capital budgeting; however, after critical examination of all methods, only the arithmetic developed in this simple model will be used to examine three methods used in evaluating capital budget proposals: (1) cash payback, (2) net present value, (3) discounted cash flow (DCF) rate of return—sometimes referred to as the "internal rate of return."

Cash payback is commonly used by businessmen evaluating investment opportunities, but it does not measure rate of return. It measures only the length of time it takes to recover the cash outlay for the investment. It indicates cash at risk. In our model there are costs of $500 committed in year 0. To determine payback we merely add the unadjusted cash flow for each year and determine how many years it takes to get the outlay back. In the first two years $450 is recovered, and by the end of the third year $600 is recovered. By interpolation we find cash recovery to be approximately 2.3 years. It is obvious that the rational businessman does not commit a large sum of money just to recover it. He expects a rate of return commensurate with the risks and his alternative use of his funds in alternative investments (opportunity cost). In our example the calculation of payback reveals a relatively short exposure of funds and cash flow continuing beyond the payback period. It is interesting information in overall project evaluation, but not con- clusive. Our model will automatically throw off payback as a by- product as we calculate the crucial time-adjusted net present value of the investment and DCF rate of return.

A version of cash payback that has come on the scene recently to aid in the evaluation of ultra-high-risk investments is described as the cash bailout method. This approach takes into account not only the annual cash flow as shown in Figure A-2, but also the estimated liquidation value of the assets at the end of each year. If the liquidation value of a highly specialized project is zero, then cash payback and cash bailout are the same. But if it is assumed in our example that the liquidation value of the investment at the end of year 1 will be $275, the cash bailout would be one year (cash flow $225 plus liquidation value $275 = $500 original cash com- mitment).

We consider net present value as described a valid basis for determining the economic consequence of an investment decision. Many business economists use it as their sole criterion for the go/ no-go decision for investment. We recognize this method as para- mount throughout our analysis but prefer using it in conjunction with other measures rather than as the sole criterion.

## Arithmetic and Concept of Discounted Cash Flow Rate of Return

We are now ready to examine the concept of DCF-ROR. It is com- pletely different from the return on investment (ROI) commonly used by businessmen. The conventional ROI is computed for an accounting period, generally on the accrual book figure; invest- ment is taken at original cost although it is sometimes taken at half original cost; no adjustment is made for time value when looked at in the long run.

We are talking about a very different rate of return on investment: The discounted cash flow rate of return is the interest rate that discounts a project's net cash flow to zero present value. Let us expand Figure A-2, which shows a $60 NPV when a discount factor of 10 percent is used, to Figure A-3, which adds a discount factor of 18 percent and yields a $0 NPV.

The DCF rate of return is 18 percent. By definition the DCF-ROR is the rate of return on the project determined by finding the interest rate at which the sum of the stream of after-tax cash flows, discounted to present worth, equals the cost of the project. Or, stated another way, the rate of return is the maximum constant rate of interest the project could pay on the investment and break even. How was the 18 percent determined? By trial and error.

There are many analysts who use the net present value method exclusively; some use the DCF rate of return; others use the two methods to complement each other. Using NPV, positive or negative dollar values are determined with the cost of capital as the benchmark. Excess dollar PV is evaluated and a judgment is made. The DCF rate of return approach ignores the cost of capital in the calculation and determines what the rate of return is on the total cash flow. The result of this approach on our example is to convert the $60 NPV into a percentage. It works out to 8 percent on top of the 10 percent that had been calculated for the NPV. Many businessmen prefer working with the single figure of 18 percent for evaluating a project against a known cost of capital, instead of describing a project as having an NPV of $60 over the cost of capital. It is our feeling that the two methods complement each other,

**Figure A-3.** Arithmetic of determining DCF rate of return.

| Year | Cash Flow | PV of $1 @ 10% | Discounted Cash Flow | PV of $1 @ 18% | Discounted Cash Flow |
|---|---|---|---|---|---|
| 0 | $(500) | 1.000 | $(500) | 1.000 | $(500) |
| 0–1 | 225 | .952 | 214 | .915 | 206 |
| 1–2 | 225 | .861 | 194 | .764 | 172 |
| 2–3 | 150 | .779 | 117 | .639 | 96 |
| 3–4 | 50 | .705 | 35 | .533 | 26 |
| TOTAL | $ 150 | | $ 60 NPV | | $ 0 NPV |

and under certain circumstances one may give a better picture than the other.

Let us reexamine this special DCF rate of return to see what distinguishes it from the conventional rate of return. It is time-adjusted to base year 0, so that all dollars are on a common denominator basis; it is calculated absolutely on a cash flow basis; the investment is a definite time-adjusted value; the rate of return is determined at a single average rate over the total life of the investment. Certain implications of this statement require explanation.

The DCF rate of return is calculated over the full life of the project, and the accountant's yearly ROI cannot be used to test the success/failure of the new investment. If the planned life of a project is ten years, and if it can be segregated from other facets of the operation, the DCF rate of return has meaning only when the full economic life of the project is completed. However, in this case it is possible to monitor results on year-to-year basis by examining the actual dollar cash flow and comparing it with the projected cash flow. (Observe the assumption that the project is separate and distinct from the rest of the operation.)

The one thing that disturbs businessmen most with the DCF rate of return concept is the underlying mathematical assumption that all cash flows are reinvested immediately and constantly at the same rate as that which yields a net present value of 0. In our example in Figure A-3, 18 percent was used as the discount factor as a constant. Another case could just as easily have indicated a 35 percent rate of return, with the implicit assumption that the cash flow was reinvested at 35 percent. But if the earning experience indicates a cost of capital of 10 percent, how can we reconcile the assumption that we can continue to earn 35 percent on the incremental flow?

Even though a company's average earnings reflect a cost of capital of 10 percent, the demands on incremental new investment may well have to be 18 to 35 percent to compensate for investments that fail to realize projected earnings. Opportunities to invest at 18 percent or 35 percent are not inconsistent with the average earnings of 10 percent. However, if it is felt that a projected rate of return of 18 percent, in our example, is a once-in-a-lifetime windfall and no new opportunities can be found to exceed the average 10 percent rate, then we are in trouble with our DCF rate of return concept.

The reinvestment rate will not stand up. In this situation we have to combine both net present value and rate of return to explain the situation in this way: The 10 percent rate of return of this project covers the opportunity cost of money and throws off an additional $60 cash flow. If other projects of the same magnitude can be found so that the total cash flow generated can be reinvested at the same rate, there would actually be a rate of return on the project of 18 percent (the DCF rate of return). The lack of other good investment opportunities is a constraint on the full earning capacity of the project.

We have examined three methods of evaluating investment opportunities. Cash payback evaluates money at risk. Present value measures the ability to cover the opportunity cost of an investment on a time-adjusted basis of money and indicates by a net present value whether the project under consideration will yeld a "profit" or a "loss." The discounted cash flow rate of return is an extension of the net present value concept and translates it into a single rate of return that when compared with the opportunity cost of capital gives a valid basis for evaluation.

Since NPV and DCF-ROR concepts take into account the opportunity cost of capital through the discounting technique, it may be stated as a principle that all projects under consideration where this opportunity cost is covered should be accepted. This proposition is both theoretically and practically sound, but three factors need to be considered: How do you determine the minimum acceptable rate of return (the opportunity cost of capital) to select the proper discounting factor? How can you assume no constraints on the supply of capital so that all worthwhile projects can be accepted? How do you take risk into account when examining indicated results. These questions will be examined in the next three sections.

## Minimum Acceptable Rate of Return—Cost of Capital

How do you determine the minimum acceptable rate of return (cost of capital) used in discounting? Again a caution: The cost of capital concept used here is not the same as the cost of borrowing. This is probably the most critical factor in the evaluation process.

It is a unique and personal rate to each company. There is no guide to look to in other companies. Two companies looking at a potential investment, say an acquisition, may place two completely different values on it. To Company A, with a minimum required rate of return of 10 percent, the investment could be attractive, while to Company B, with a required rate of return of 25 percent, the investment would be totally unacceptable. The difference is centered in the cost of capital to each company, its opportunity rate of return—the rate that can be expected on alternative investments having similar risk characteristics. An example of the arithmetic involved in reaching this conclusion can be seen when we modify Figure A-2 to include both a 10 percent and 25 percent discount factor and assume that both companies A and B are the potential sole bidders for an investment with an asked price of $500 and a net cash flow of $150 (see Figure A-4).

The investment is very attractive to Company A but completely unacceptable to Company B—it would realize less than its objective of 25 percent. If Company A were in a position to know the cost of capital of Company B, it would know that Company B would not bid at all for this investment. Company A would know that it would be the sole bidder.

If a company has successfully earned 25 percent on the capital employed in it, for an investment opportunity to be attractive it would have to yield at least that rate. The 25 percent represents the cost of capital to that company and an investment opportunity

**Figure A-4.** Comparison of NPV using 10 percent and 25 percent discount factors.

| | | (A) | | (B) | |
|---|---|---|---|---|---|
| Year | Cash Flow | PV of $1 @ 10% | Discounted Cash Flow | PV of $1 @ 25% | Discounted Cash Flow |
| 0 | $(500) | 1.000 | $(500) | 1.000 | $(500) |
| 1 | 225 | .952 | 214 | .885 | 199 |
| 2 | 225 | .861 | 194 | .689 | 155 |
| 3 | 150 | .779 | 117 | .537 | 81 |
| 4 | 50 | .705 | 35 | .418 | 21 |
| TOTAL | $ 150 | | $ 60 NPV | | $ (44) NPV |

offering only 15 percent would be rejected. A second company with a 10 percent cost of capital would find the same 15 percent potential attractive and accept it. Thus the same 15 percent opportunity investment is attractive to one and unattractive to the other. Both companies analyzing the identical situation reach different logical conclusions.

Cost of capital in our analysis is *always* considered to be the combined cost of equity capital and permanent debt. We evaluate economic success/failure of a project without regard to how it is financed. Yet we know that money available for investment is basically derived from two sources: debt with its built-in tax saving so that its cost is half the market price for money (assuming a 50 percent tax rate), and equity, which has as its cost the opportunity cost of capital of the owners.

It is necessary at times to break down the combined cost of capital into its components of cost of debt capital and cost of equity capital to put it in terms understandable to the businessman who commonly measures results in terms of return on equity. To illustrate this cost of capital concept, we will assume that a corporation is owned by a single individual whose investment objectives are clearly defined. The total capitalization of the company is $100, made up of $30 permanent debt capital and $70 owner's equity capital. If preferred stock was outstanding at a fixed cost, it would be treated the same as debt. The after-tax interest rate of the debt money is 2.75 percent. The after-tax dollar return on the combined debt and equity capital of $100 under various operations would appear as shown in Figure A-5.

To restate these dollars as rates of return on the investment of $100, $30 debt, and $70 equity, the percentage return on capital would be as shown in Figure A-6.

If the company has been earning an average of $10 on the total investment of $100, and the cost of debt is $.825, the earning on owner's equity is $9.175. Stated as a rate of return, the $10 earned on $100 is 10 percent return on the total investment (combined cost of capital), and because of the leverage built into the capital structure with long-term debt, the $9.175 earning on equity yields a return on equity of 13.11 percent (cost of equity capital). When there is a 30 percent debt structure and the average cost of debt is 2.75 percent after taxes, we can readily convert return on total

**Figure A-5.** After-tax dollar income on investment of $100.

| Income on Total Investment (Before Interest) | $30 Debt × 2.75% Cost of Debt Capital | $70 Equity Income on Owner's Equity |
|---|---|---|
| $ 8.00 | $0.825 | $ 7.175 |
| 9.00 | 0.825 | 8.175 |
| 10.00 | 0.825 | 9.175 |
| 11.00 | 0.825 | 10.175 |
| 12.00 | 0.825 | 11.175 |

**Figure A-6.** After-tax rate of return on investment of $100.

| Rate of Return | Cost of Debt Capital | Rate of Return on Owner's Equity |
|---|---|---|
| 8% | 2.75% ($0.825 ÷ $30) | 10.25% ($7.175 ÷ $70) |
| 9 | 2.75 | 11.68 |
| 10 | 2.75 | 13.11 |
| 11 | 2.75 | 14.54 |
| 12 | 2.75 | 15.96 |

investment into return on equity by reading our table. It is quite simple to create similar tables for each company and its debt/equity ratio (e.g., with a 50/50 ratio and debt cost of 2.75 percent, a 10 percent return on total investment yields a 17.45 percent return on equity capital). If there is the opportunity to invest the company funds in alternative situations or reinvest the funds in the business and continue to earn at least 10 percent on the combined debt/equity funds, we would describe this as the opportunity cost of capital. This is the critical rate used in discounting: The discount rate used to determine net present value and the benchmark for comparing discounted cash flow rate of return are based solely on the combined cost of capital. The rate of return to the stockholders can be derived and compared with their opportunity cost, that is, their ability to invest their funds elsewhere and earn at least the same rate.

Having decided that return on combined capital is the appropriate criterion for evaluating investment, it is necessary to follow through with this concept when projecting revenues, expenses, and net benefits. If we are to determine net benefits (cash flow) on combined capital, all charges against that capital must be excluded from the expense projections. If interest were charged in the projection, there would be double charging. This is not a novel method; it is used regularly by investment analysts who often determine income before interest on funded debt and before taxes.

As noted, interest expense on long-term debt is not included in the current expense projection because it is covered in the combined cost of capital computation. The interest on short-term debt may be a direct charge to operations if its cost is not in the invested capital base. If the major financing is handled through equity and long-term debt and the short-term borrowing is negligible, this method is acceptable. However, many companies live off their current borrowings and the short-term debt is actually part of the permanent capital. The true leverage would then be reflected in the return on owner's equity when compared with the return on total investment. Once more, a caution: When this method is used, the interest expense on current debt must be excluded from projected costs.

The capital funds of a company constitute a pool of monies for all projects. A particular borrowing rate for additional capital, at a time when a new project is introduced, becomes part of the pool of funds and it becomes part of the average cost of debt relative to total capital. With the addition of new funds, it is the average long-run cost that is significant and not the current borrowing rate. The relevant comparison of the projected rate of return is with the average rate for the pool of funds and not the cost of the incremental funds.

In the case of the individual ownership of a corporation, the historical earnings rate can be determined along these lines and a cost of capital for opportunity cost evaluation can become a valid benchmark. If average earnings rise from $10 to $12, there is a new cost of capital, a new cutoff rate for accepting or rejecting projects. This does not imply constantly changing cutoff rates. Some years will be more profitable than other years, some years the cost of debt may be higher or lower than other years, but the earnings of the company are the average adjusted for trend. There is not much logic in setting a cutoff rate at 25 percent when the average is 10 percent, just because there was once an isolated year that had unusually high earnings. Many good projects would be rejected because of an unrealistically high cutoff point. The reference point should be actual accomplishment and reasonable expectations, not wishful thinking.

When the assumption of the individual ownership of a corporation is abandoned in favor of a public corporation with myriad stockholders, the cost of capital concept gets into difficulty. It is difficult enough postulating the opportunity cost of capital for even a small family, but when we try to postulate the investment objectives of all the different stockholers in a large corporation, things become really complex. One stockholder wants cash dividends; another wants growth and reinvestment of earnings; still another wants fast capital appreciation. The opportunity cost of capital to each owner goes undetermined. We are not going to grapple with the problem of cost of capital for publicly owned corporations here, because it is a problem that is extremely complex and can be highly theoretical. It is sufficient to note that some large public corporations have been able to develop a cost of capital for their capital budgeting evaluations with some success. Other public corporations have conceded that they cannot develop a cost of capital for all their stockholders and have resorted to a cutoff rate commensurate with their earnings experience. This latter approach violates the opportunity cost concept for the individual owners, but practical considerations have made it necessary to recognize the opportunity cost of the corporation as a person with only minor reference to the real persons who own it.

## Constraints on Supply of Capital

How can you assume no constraints on supply of capital for investment? Theoretically, if the earnings of a corporation are great enough and growing fast enough, there is no limit on the amount of debt and equity available. In good basic economic theory, companies should continue their capital expansion until the marginal cost of capital equals its marginal revenue; or stated simply, it is worth borrowing as long as the earnings exceed the cost by even a small amount. The principal limit on debt to the successful corporation becomes the ability of the management to live with it—at what point do the managers start losing sleep because they are so heavily leveraged? However, there are other practical constraints. General business conditions and the state of optimism/pessimism may lead to a limit on the amount of capital a management is willing to commit. There are constraints on the amount of risk a management may be willing to assume; there may be limits on the ability of an organization to handle certain ventures. There are probably other constraints, real and imaginary. In the budgeting process all categories of investments must be classified and weighed. The degree of risk willing to be assumed, and a commensurate return, is something that exists only in the mind of individual managements.

There is no nice formula that can set this. Depending on the management's philosophy, and assuming constraints on availability of capital, the selection may result in the rejection of good safe investments promising a 10 percent return, and acceptance of promotional investments with a great risk promising a 60 percent return, and vice versa. Another constraint mentioned is organization, which may be the decisive factor in choosing between an investment that will make few demands on management and one that will make great demands on management. The latter may offer a superior projected return, yet it may be rejected, reluctantly, because management does not have confidence in its ability to cope with it even though the indicated economic rewards are greater. The practical problems of project selection are varied and complex. While the techniques discussed are hardly the *sine qua non,* they do lend objectivity and direction.

## Describing Risk and Uncertainty

How do you account for risk in evaluating the net present value or DCF rate of return? A more accurate term is uncertainty, but risk and uncertainty tend to be used interchangeably by businessmen. The technical difference between the two terms is found in the ability to determine probability of future outcome. Risk, with respect to outcome, implies that future events can be determined within a range of known probabilities, while uncertainty implies that probabilities of outcome cannot be established. Not all proposals have exactly the same element of risk. One investment risk category, the outlay of funds to introduce labor-saving equipment, can be evaluated quite accurately; the projected benefits may be almost a certainty.

Management could even decide to accept all such proposals where indicated NPV exceeds the combined cost of capital. Another category of risk may be the introduction of new product lines. The difference in uncertainty between the two categories is obvious. There probably would be no blanket acceptance of proposals for new products at the cost of capital cutoff rate.

The discount factor remains constant no matter what the risk. The recognition of the different risk categories results in a subjective evaluation of the uncertainties of the venture and a markup on the cost of capital for the go/no-go decision. For example, with a cost of capital of 10 percent, a proposal is made to invest in replacement equipment. There is a modest NPV, little uncertainty. All such proposals would be segregated and acted upon and probably accepted. The second situation, introducing a completely new line or lines whose success is highly uncertain and producing a modest positive NPV, would hardly be acceptable. All such risky proposals would be segregated and judged individually within this special group. To compensate for the uncertainty, a minimum acceptable cutoff rate may be two or three times the cost of capital rate. Average success/failure may actually fall to the 10 percent average cost of capital to the company.

The determination of the projected rate of return on an investment from the NPV can be arrived at by raising the discount rate until the NPV is zero. This is the DCF rate of return, which is the projected average return on the investment. If such a rate came to 18 percent against a cost of capital of 10 percent, it is still left to the judgment of management whether the additional 8 percent rate of return is adequate to cover the uncertainty of success/failure. This is how risk is usually evaluated—purely subjectively.

There are more exact and sophisticated methods that we will describe. Risk implies probabilities of success/failure. The fact that the project evaluation method we describe here is quite precise and yields a definite answer must not blind us to the reality that decisions are always made in the face of uncertainty. The rate of return description of a project's economic consequences is a single, uncertain prediction of projected revenues and expenses. We cannot ever completely remove this uncertainty. The best we can do is to describe the probable range and intensity of uncertainty involved and the economic consequences of forecasting errors. Next, we briefly discuss three methods that have been found helpful in performing this work.

### Sensitivity Analysis

Sensitivity analysis seeks to determine how much a project's net present value or DCF rate of return will be affected (its "sensitivity") when a single factor, or specific group of factors, changes by a given amount. Let's say that for a given project we have been able to predict the volume of product sales with relative certainty, but the price forecast remains very doubtful. To make a sensitivity analysis, we would repeat the evaluation using different prices; this would show how much the NPV changes with each price change.

When used with discretion, the results of sensitivity analyses are helpful in estimating the economic consequences of specific forecasting errors. As a minimum requirement, each project evaluation should describe the effect of a wrong forecast in the factor or factors judged most uncertain. However, with analysis of this type we are measuring the effect of change of a single factor or group of factors while all other factors in the projection are held constant. When other components of the projection change, and they are ignored, the new answers may have serious limitations. For example, to change projected prices but to hold volume and costs constant may be unrealistic. We become "practical" at this point and settle for simple sensitivity analysis and get rough answers, because manually reworking the model to reflect all possible changes in the figures to determine new cash flows becomes an almost impossible task. In this area computer programs really become significant. Hundreds of single factors can be tested against all other factors and the arithmetic can be worked accurately in minutes instead of in weeks.

## Probability Adjustment

Probability is the preferred method of organizing estimates of both the range and intensity of uncertainty for the decision maker. In using this method the decision maker computes a reasonable range of possible outcomes for the economic model from very unfavorable to very favorable. From them, it is possible to estimate the probability that each will occur. If the unfavorable outcome seems more likely than the favorable one, the project is probably unwise, and vice versa.

An example of probability analysis after the initial projection has been made can be prepared as a test of its validity. No one can forecast with complete confidence and certainty the annual cash flows resulting from projected volume, prices, or even costs. The probability of achievement can be examined by preparing a table of possible deviations from the forecast. Assuming the initial annual cash flows had been projected at $10,000, a reappraisal by management might indicate the following possible results:

5 chances in 100 annual cash flow will be $14,000
25 chances in 100 annual cash flow will be $12,000
45 chances in 100 annual cash flow will be $10,000
20 chances in 100 annual cash flow will be $ 8,000
5 chances in 100 annual cash flow will be $     0

It is apparent that the projected $10,000 annual cash flow has been reassessed as being the most probable, and there is also an indication of a 30 percent chance that it will be exceeded. However, there is a 20 percent chance that it will be less, and a 5 percent chance that it will fail completely.

There is no precise formula for testing the validity of the judgments that lead to predictions of chances of success/failure. They are based upon subjective judgments of experienced and responsible executives. If this type of analysis does nothing more than force an orderly reappraisal of a project, it will serve its purpose. In this example, the conclusion may be that the $10,000 annual cash flow forecast looks reasonable and the initial projection would be allowed to stand. If, on the other hand, the probabilities of achieving less than the $10,000 had been greater, it would probably lead to a write-down of the cash flows.

The introduction of probability analysis also opens the way to very sophisticated statistical analysis of projected results. Computer programs have been developed that measure probabilities of success/failure of the principal factors making up the projection (volume, prices, costs), and it is possible to determine projected results by taking into account any combination of favorable and unfavorable events. The DCF rate of return is then stated as rates over a range of probabilities.

## Project Evaluation

Evaluating components of an investment program for a company is complex at any time. There are many categories of investment: (1) revenue-producing projects, (2) supporting facilities projects, (3) supporting services projects, (4) cost-savings projects, and (5) last but hardly least, in this era of air and water pollution control, investment required by public authority that will yield no return. Each must be evaluated to determine its incremental consequences.

When a project is isolated from the rest of the operation, evaluation is relatively clear. But sometimes a planned major investment embraces several auxiliary projects which, evaluated by themselves, are not very meaningful. When this occurs, it is necessary to construct a master model that includes all of the projects. Some of the auxiliary projects may not come into being for several years after the main investment is made, and may or may not produce a new positive cash flow. The master model in simple form may take on the appearance shown in Figure A-7 if individual projects of the

**Figure A-7.** Master project.

| Project | NPV | 0 | 1 | 2 | 3 | 4 | 5 | ... | 15 |
|---------|-----|-----|-----|------|-----|-----|-----|-----|------|
| (a) | 100 | (30) | (2) | 14 | 14 | 13 | 13 | | 40 |
| (b) | 40 | — | — | (15) | 5 | 5 | 5 | | 20 |
| (c) | (26) | — | (2) | (2) | (4) | (4) | (4) | | (10) |
| TOTAL | 114 | (30) | (4) | (3) | 15 | 14 | 14 | | (50) |

types (a), (b), and (c) are assumed (the figures do not add up—only format is demonstrated).

If the three projects are interrelated, they should be projected as a single entity. In our example, (a) is assumed to be a major facility that to be successful needs (b) added in three years as supporting facilities; (b) would have no basis for existence if (a) were not created. Project (c) may possibly be identified as a new computer/information system that will produce only costs, but would not exist if (a) and (b) were not created. All costs and all benefits for all corollary investments need to be projected as far into the future as possible to get a true evaluation. Investment evaluations that are made of a project with all the certainty of a DCF percentage can be grossly misleading if the supporting investment of satellites is not taken into account. Actually, these are not separate investments. There is only one—Project abc. The evaluation has to be of the new single entity. The postaudit can be of only the conglomerate single entity (abc).

Projects of the cost-savings category are generally easiest to identify and evaluate. There are relatively clear-cut choices: Invest $40,000 today for new labor-saving machines that will reduce labor costs $12,000 per year; the machines will last eight years, and quality of performance will be unchanged. Determine the NPV and/or DCF rate of return and accept/reject. Such investment opportunities constantly arise, but it is almost impossible to project them as part of a master project. As a result, such investments are evaluated as isolated investment opportunities that may occur in three years, or eight years, or never. When they occur, if of major proportions, they affect the potential return on the total investment.

A cost-incurring project, such as spend $100,000 to prevent air pollution or be closed up, is one of the few black-and-white decisions a manager faces. Ideally it would be expensed. It may have to be capitalized and written off and in addition have annual related operating expenses. This nondiscretionary investment falls into the same general category as support project. The cash flow is always negative and must be included as an integral part of the master investment. A large enough commitment may sharply reduce the original projection and a revision may be necessary.

### Selecting Among Projects

On the basis of the techniques for evaluating planned capital investment, it is now possible to move to the methods of selecting among projects. As noted above, in theory, selecting among projects is easy. Invest in anything that when discounted at the appropriate marginal rate will yield a positive NPV. Practically, for many reasons, there are constraints on capital in the minds of most managers. Let us look at the project selection problems that are involved for projects under consideration in a particular risk category when there is a limit on capital.

We have selected the NPV method as the best approach to analyze proposed projects of varying lives. Comparing projects under the DCF-ROR method can be misleading because of the different life factor and the reinvestment factor inherent in each ROR. Excess NPV avoids this difficulty. When the various projects are converted into a profitability index, selection is further facilitated. The profitability index is the ratio of the NPV to investment. For example:

$$\frac{\text{Present value of expected benefits}}{\text{Investment}} = \frac{\$132,000}{\$100,000} = 1.32$$

In selecting projects when a limit is imposed upon the amount available for investment, we look for the combination that will maximize combined net present value without exceeding the imposed limit. We know that we have reached this goal when we can no longer increase the combined net present value by substituting one project for another and still satisfy the constraint.

A way to achieve a satisfactory combination of projects is through trial and error. As a guide we can use the profitability index (see Figure A-8). However, such ratios are not foolproof. This is illustrated where there are three possible projects requiring a total of $1,500 in initial outlays, but where $1,000 is the imposed limit.

The choice is between investment in A + C (cash outlay $1,000) or investment B + C (cash outlay $900). Since A + C has a combined greater NPV than B + C ($1,500 vs. $1,200), A + C

**Figure A-8.** Profitability index.

| Project | Net Present Value | ÷ | Investment: Cash Outlay | = | Profit-ability Index |
|---------|---|---|---|---|---|
| A | $1,000 | | $600 | | 1.67 |
| B | 700 | | 500 | | 1.40 |
| C | 500 | | 400 | | 1.25 |

should be selected even though C's ratio (1.25) is less than B's ratio (1.40). Such differences are common. The profitability index must always be used judiciously. When there are numerous projects to choose among, the combining process becomes more difficult.

## Summary

Top management's capital budgeting process always starts with the formula

$$\text{Benefits} - \text{costs} = \text{cash flow}$$

This is the basis for preparing all projections. The next step is to adjust the cash flow to eliminate time differences. All cash flows are adjusted to year 0, which becomes the common denominator for evaluations. The adjustment is made by discounting future values to present values. The mechanics of discounting are not difficult to master but the determination of a discount factor is. The discount factor is the interest rate that equates with the company's combined cost of capital. This is a relatively new concept and should not be confused with the traditional cost of borrowing. Cost of capital is the rate earned on the combined capital of equity holders plus the permanent debt used as part of the capital of the company. This simple explanation stands up for the company with a sole owner who can evaluate the rate of return with his own opportunity cost of capital. When a public corporation becomes involved, the calculation of equity cost of capital could become extremely complex if an attempt were made to take into account the opportunity costs of the various stockholders. For our examination we have simplified the problem by recognizing a combined cost of capital where the opportunity costs can be determined. This rate becomes the discount value and is used for discounting.

When proposed investment benefits are discounted at a rate consistent with cost of capital, we have a net present value that tells us that the project will yield more or less than the cost of capital. This rate becomes our cutoff rate when we consider whether to accept or reject. Many analysts use this NPV as the sole criterion for evaluation of the project. We recognize the importance of NPV but carry it a step further to discounted cash flow rate of return (DCF-ROR), because the latter changes the excess NPV dollars to a single percentage rate of return that is often easier to comprehend. These two measuring devices that are time-adjusted through the discounting methodology are teamed up with several other criteria to bring the maximum information to bear on the analysis. The most prominent of these is cash payback, which is introduced to reflect money at risk only, and not a rate of return. All these calculations were built on judgments by responsible executives. The final calculations are presented to a budget committee for its appraisal of the facts. The validity of the mathematics used in the projection and final evaluation is dependent on the skill, objectivity, and integrity of the people making the multitude of subjective judgments that are needed at many stages in the development of the projection.

When an NPV or DCF-ROR is determined for a project, and if the company's alternative to investment is to do nothing, the choice is clear. When the choice of capital commitment is among several projects and there is a limit on the amount of capital available for investment, we have chosen to compare projects using NPV rather than DCF-ROR. We are not committed to saying NPV is better than DCF-ROR in all situations, or vice versa. Each has features that work better in some situations.

We recognize the need to control authorized cash expenditures once a commitment is made. Projections of NPV or rate of return are made. If cash expenditures exceed estimates, the projected benefits are meaningless. Practically, this has been a pitfall for many good capital budgeting procedures. If large overexpenditures are made, a new projection should be prepared; however, this only yields a new rate of return after the fact. By that time we are merely generating statistics.

Postaudit of investment is difficult. It is often neglected. If a plan of postaudit is not determined and agreed upon at the time a commitment is to be made, the probabilities are there won't be one or a postaudit will be attempted and it may not be satisfactory. As all investments are projected on an incremental basis, and the results are usually part of a larger investment, there is an inability to sort out the results of the incremental portion and identify its NPV or DCF-ROR. It is not fair to management, and it is poor budgeting procedure, to establish a value upon which important decisions are made and then announce you cannot compare the results with the budget. NPV and DCF-ROR indicate expected results over the complete life of the investment, but there is a desire and need to appraise results on an annual basis. For those investments that can be identified apart from other investments, the postaudit can be in the form of tests of cash flow and adjusted financial statements. When the investment becomes an integral part of existing investments, the incremental portion cannot be identified and plans must be made to postaudit on the basis of the new combined investment.

# Appendix B

# How Top Managers Choose Lease vs. Buy

Leasing is an alternative to ownership that allows managers to free themselves from the owner's risks of maintenance and obsolescence. Risk reduction has a price in the rental payments on the lease. Managers who want to run their businesses as close as possible to "zero assets" accept this tradeoff. Managers who prefer to maintain a high degree of control over their businesses may reject leasing for ownership whether or not it is cost-effective.

## Outright Purchase vs. Long-Term Lease

The decision to buy or lease can be made only after a systematic evaluation of the relevant factors. The evaluation must be carried out in two stages: First, the advantages and disadvantages of purchase or lease must be considered, and, second, the cash flows under both alternatives must be compared.

Figure B-1 shows the principal advantages and disadvantages of leasing from both the lessor's and lessee's standpoint. This listing is only a guide. For both parties, the relative significance of the advantages and disadvantages depends on many factors. Major determinants are a company's size, financial position, and tax status. For example, to a heavily leveraged public company, the disadvantage of having to record additional debt may be consider-

*(text continues on page 142)*

From Mack Hanan, *Consultative Selling*™ (New York: AMACOM, 1991), adapted from "Leasing vs. Buying," *The Lybrand Journal*, Fall 1972, and reprinted by permission of Coopers & Lybrand.

**Figure B-1.**   Leasing advantages and disadvantages.

---

**Lessee Advantages**

- *One hundred percent financing of the cost of the property (the lease is based on the full cost) on terms that may be individually tailored to the lessee.*
- *Possible avoidance of existing loan indenture restrictions on new debt financing.* Free of these restrictions, the lessee may be able to increase his base, as lease obligations are generally not reflected on the balance sheet, although the lease obligation will probably require footnote disclosure in the financial statements. (It should be noted, however, that a number of the more recent loan indentures restrict lease commitments.)
- *General allowability of rental deductions for the term of the lease, without problems or disputes about the property's depreciable life.*
- *Possibly higher net book income during the earlier years of the basic lease term than under outright ownership.* Rental payments in the lease's earlier years are generally lower than the combined interest expense and depreciation (even on the straight-line method) that a corporate property owner would otherwise have charged in the income statement.
- *Potential reduction in state and city franchise and income taxes.* The property factor, which is generally one of the three factors in the allocation formula, is reduced.
- *Full deductibility of rent payment.* This is true notwithstanding the fact that the rent is partially based on the cost of the land.

**Lessee Disadvantages**

- *Loss of residual rights to the property upon the lease's termination.* When the lessee has full residual rights, the transaction cannot be a true lease; instead, it is a form of financing. In a true lease, the lessee may have the right to purchase or renew, but the exercise of these options requires payments to the lessor after the full cost of the property has been amortized.
- *Rentals greater than comparable debt service.* Since the lessor generally borrows funds with which to buy the asset to be leased, the rent is based on the lessor's debt service plus a profit factor. This amount may exceed the debt service that the lessee would have had to pay had he purchased the property.

- *Loss of operating and financing flexibility.* If an asset were owned outright and a new, improved model became available, the owner could sell or exchange the old model for the new one. This may not be possible under a lease. Moreover, if interest rates decreased, the lessee would have to continue paying at the old rate, whereas the owner of the asset could refinance his debt at a lower rate.
- *Loss of tax benefits from accelerated depreciation and high interest deductions in early years.* These benefits would produce a temporary cash saving if the property were purchased instead of leased.

## Lessor Advantages

- *Higher rate of return than on investment in straight debt.* To compensate for risk and lack of marketability, the lessor can charge the lessee a higher effective rate—particularly after considering the lessor's tax benefits—than the lessor could obtain by lending the cost of the property at the market rate.
- *The lessor has the leased asset as security.* Should the lessee have financial trouble, the lessor can reclaim a specific asset instead of having to take his place with the general creditors.
- *Retention of the property's residual value upon the lease's termination.* The asset's cost is amortized over the basic lease term. If, upon the lease's expiration, the lessee abandons the property, the lessor can sell it. If the lessee renews or purchases, the proceeds to the lessor represent substantially all profit.

## Lessor Disadvantages

- *Dependence upon lessee's ability to maintain payments on a timely basis.*
- *Vulnerability to unpredictable changes in the tax law that (1) reduce tax benefits and related cash flow or (2) significantly extend depreciable life.* The latter measure would lessen the projected return upon which the lessor based his investment.
- *Probable negative after-tax cash flow in later years.* As the lease progresses, an increasing percentage of the rent goes toward nondeductible amortization of the principal. Both the interest and depreciation deductions (under the accelerated method) decline as the lease progresses.
- *Potentially large tax on disposition of asset imposed by the Internal Revenue Code's depreciation recapture provisions.*

able, even critical; the disadvantage may be insignificant to a privately held concern.

## Analysis of Cash Flows

A cash flow analysis enables the potential lessee to contrast his cash position under both buying and leasing. This is essentially a capital budgeting procedure, and the method of developing and comparing cash flows should conform to the company's capital budgeting policies and practices. There are several comparison criteria in current use, among which the three commonest are rate of return, discounted cash flow, and net cash position.

1. *Outright purchase.* The cash outflows in an outright purchase are the initial purchase price or, assuming the asset is purchased with borrowed funds, as is almost always the case, the subsequent principal and interest on the loan. There will also be operating expenses, such as maintenance and insurance, but these items are excluded from the comparison because they will be the same under both purchase and leasing, assuming a net lease. The charge for depreciation is a noncash item. Cash inflows are the amount of the loan, the tax benefit from the yearly interest and depreciation, and the salvage value, if any.

2. *Leasing.* The lessee's cash flows are easier to define than the buyer's. The lessee pays a yearly rental, which is fully deductible. The lessee will thus have level annual outflows offset by the related tax benefit over the lease period. Salvage or residual value does not enter the picture because the lessee generally has no right of ownership in the asset.

3. *Comparing the cash flows.* Once the annual cash flows from outright purchase and leasing have been developed, the next step is to contrast the flows by an accepted method (such as discounted cash flow) to determine which alternative gives the greater cash benefit or yield. In so doing, some consideration must be given to the effects of changes in the assumptions adopted. Examples could include a lengthening by the IRS of the depreciation period or a change in interest rates. In this manner, a series of contingencies

could be introduced into the analysis, as follows: Assume a ten-year life and a borrowing at 10 percent. If outright purchase is better by $x$ dollars, then:

- A two-year increase in depreciable life reduces the benefit of outright purchase to $(x\text{-}y)$ dollars.
- An upward change in interest rate reduces the benefit of outright purchase to $(x\text{-}z)$ dollars.

Probabilities could be assigned to the contingencies, for example: that the depreciable life could be extended by two years, 30 percent; or that interest rates could rise by one half a percentage point, 10 percent. Once the contingencies have been quantified, an overall probability of achieving the expected saving can then be calculated.

It must be stressed that the rate of return—the product of the cash-flow analysis—is not the exclusive or even, in some cases, the main determinant in deciding whether to buy or lease. Such factors as impact on financial statements, desire for operational flexibility, and loan restrictions, as well as other accounting, tax, economic, and financial considerations, may be collectively at least as important. These aspects are essentially nonquantitative, but they can be evaluated with a satisfactory degree of accuracy by weighing the advantages and disadvantages.

## Tax Considerations

There are two ways in which a lease can be treated for tax purposes, as a true lease or as a form of financing. If the lease is viewed as a true lease, the lessee is entitled to a deduction, in the appropriate period, for his annual rental expenses. (Normally, the appropriate period is the period in which the liability for rent is incurred, in accordance with the terms of the lease, granted that the timing of the liability is not unreasonable.) If the lease is viewed as a form of financing, the lessee is deemed the property's equitable owner and is thus permitted to deduct the depreciation and interest expense.

The test the IRS applies to determine whether a lease is a true lease or a form of financing is basically an evaluation of the purchase options. If the lessee can purchase the property for less than the fair market value or for an amount approximately equal to what the debt balance would have been had the asset been bought outright, the transaction is viewed as a financing agreement. If the lessee has a purchase option in an amount substantially exceeding the probable fair market value or the debt balance, the transaction would probably be recognized as a lease.

# Index